LESSONS LEARNED

Advance Praise for *Lessons Learned*

"There is no better approach to education and training than student staff teaching student staff. John has turned an educational method into a training model for Resident Assistants. *Lessons Learned* guides staff through real situations offering great approaches and opportunity for discussion. All Resident Assistants and their supervisors will grow tremendously from utilizing the approach and techniques in *Lessons Learned*."

—**Norbert W. Dunkel**, Director of Housing and Residence Education,
University of Florida

"What a terrific book! The format is easy to read and very personal for RAs who will use it. The 'lessons learned' are all true-to-life and current RAs will certainly be able to relate to them. I expect we'll be able to use this for staff training in lots of different ways. It will be a great learning tool!"

—**Julie Weber**, Executive Director of Housing and Dining Programs,
American University

"During my extensive time as an RA, I was confronted with a wide and diverse range of issues of varying degrees and severity. The available 'resources' at the time were haphazardly and glibly prepared (often from the perspective of someone who was never an RA) wherein I found myself re-inventing the wheel, even for the most mundane issues. Having been through the trenches, I can say that Foubert has compiled a comprehensive treatise addressing all of the issues an RA will encounter with real-life examples. There is now only one definitive guide for each and every RA to own, and it is *Lessons Learned*."

—**Michael A. Sauer**, former RA, Johns Hopkins University Class of 2002

"Dr. Foubert's book *Lessons Learned* offers its readers a creative way to consider and discuss important issues with residence hall staff members. This innovative approach—the presentation of letters to new staff members from a current staff member—offers a non-threatening way for staff to tackle and talk about issues from first-year students to facebook concerns from programming to parents and multi-culturalism to multi-tasking. In addition to the 'letter' that describes each situation there are tips for the journey and resources, mostly web-based, that make this a very contemporary source for current staff members."

—**Jeanne S. Steffes**, Ph.D., President, ACPA- College Student Educators
International Associate Vice President, Syracuse University

"Dr. Foubert captures the essence and complexity of the RA position and the folksy language made the book fun to read. Housing professionals and their RAs will benefit from the discussion questions and the 'Tips' are solid and helpful."

—**Deb Boykin**, Assistant Vice President for Student Affairs and Director of
Residence Life, College of William and Mary

"Foubert weaves real-life mistakes together with insight, seeking help, and second chances to provide an extremely helpful guide for Resident Assistants. Leadership learning is frequently most powerful when it includes reflection on the leadership initiatives that have not gone as well as we hoped; this book captures this powerful dynamic in wonderful ways."

—**Denny Roberts**, Associate Vice President for Student Affairs,
Miami University

LESSONS LEARNED

How to Avoid the Biggest Mistakes
Made by College Resident Assistants

John D. Foubert

Routledge
Taylor & Francis Group
New York   London

Routledge is an imprint of the
Taylor & Francis Group, an informa business

Routledge
Taylor & Francis Group
270 Madison Avenue
New York, NY 10016

Routledge
Taylor & Francis Group
2 Park Square
Milton Park, Abingdon
Oxon OX14 4RN

© 2007 by Taylor & Francis Group, LLC
Routledge is an imprint of Taylor & Francis Group, an Informa business

Printed in the United States of America on acid-free paper
10 9 8 7 6 5 4 3 2

International Standard Book Number-10: 0-415-95468-1 (Softcover)
International Standard Book Number-13: 978-0-415-95468-6 (Softcover)

Library of Congress Cataloging-in-Publication Data

Foubert, John.
   Lessons learned : how to avoid the biggest mistakes made by college resident assistants / John D. Foubert.
      p. cm.
   ISBN 0-415-95468-1 (pb)
   1. Resident assistants (Dormitories)--Vocational guidance. 2. Dormitory life. I. Title.

LB3227.F68 2006
378.1'12--dc22   2006030861

Visit the Taylor & Francis Web site at
http://www.taylorandfrancis.com

and the Routledge Web site at
http://www.routledgementalhealth.com

Contents

ABOUT THE AUTHOR IX

PREFACE XI

ACKNOWLEDGMENTS XV

PART 1 BUILDING COMMUNITY: THE BASICS 1

CHAPTER 1 BEING AWAY A LOT FROM THE FLOOR DURING
THE FIRST WEEK OF SCHOOL 3

CHAPTER 2 WAITING UNTIL THE SECOND MONTH OF THE
YEAR TO DO PROGRAMMING 7

CHAPTER 3 PLANNING AN EVENT WITH YOUR HALL
COUNCIL AND DOING ALL THE WORK YOURSELF 11

CHAPTER 4 AVOIDING CONFLICT: SEEING IT AS HARMFUL
TO COMMUNITY 17

CHAPTER 5 JUMPING INTO SERVICE WITHOUT LEARNING 23

CHAPTER 6 HELPING STUDENTS CHOOSE THEIR FRIENDS
CAREFULLY: AVOIDING CULTS 29

PART 2 BUILDING AN INCLUSIVE COMMUNITY 35

CHAPTER 7 ASSUMING STUDENTS IN A RACIAL MINORITY
DON'T WANT TO PARTICIPATE IN HALL
ACTIVITIES 37

CHAPTER 8 TRYING TO HELP A STUDENT OF A DIFFERENT
RACE AND MAKING THINGS WORSE 43

CHAPTER 9 IGNORING RACIST COMMENTS 49

CHAPTER 10 A CASE OF RELIGIOUS DISCRIMINATION 55

CHAPTER 11 THE FACEBOOK NIGHTMARE 61

PART 3 RESIDENT SUPPORT 67

CHAPTER 12 ASSUMING THAT A FIRST-YEAR STUDENT WHO OUTWARDLY SEEMS TO HAVE IT ALL TOGETHER DOESN'T NEED ANY HELP OR SUPPORT 69

CHAPTER 13 NOT CONFRONTING A STUDENT WHO SERVES OTHERS SO MUCH THAT SHE HURTS HERSELF 73

CHAPTER 14 NOT REACHING OUT TO A LONELY RESIDENT 77

CHAPTER 15 TELLING A RESIDENT'S PARENT THAT IT IS OK TO CALL YOU 83

CHAPTER 16 COMMUNICATING WITH A RESIDENT OVER INSTANT MESSENGER INSTEAD OF HAVING A CONVERSATION IN PERSON 87

CHAPTER 17 KEEPING YOUR RELATIONSHIPS WITH RESIDENTS IN BALANCE 91

PART 4 POLICY ENFORCEMENT 97

CHAPTER 18 "IF I CAN'T SEE IT, IT ISN'T THERE": A DANGEROUS WAY TO AVOID POLICY ENFORCEMENT 99

CHAPTER 19 ENJOYING POLICY ENFORCEMENT TOO MUCH 105

CHAPTER 20 ENFORCING POLICY SELECTIVELY: HOW TO REALLY ANNOY YOUR RESIDENTS 111

CHAPTER 21 IGNORING ESCALATING DOMESTIC VIOLENCE 115

CHAPTER 22 ASSUMING A RESIDENT WHO COMES HOME DRUNK FREQUENTLY CAN HANDLE THEIR ALCOHOL 121

CHAPTER 23 ASSUMING THAT ALL STUDENTS WHO APPEAR INTOXICATED WERE DRINKING ALCOHOL AND NOT USING OTHER DRUGS 125

PART 5 HELPING STUDENTS WITH PSYCHOLOGICAL DIFFICULTIES 131

CHAPTER 24 PROMISING A RESIDENT YOU WON'T TELL ANYONE WHAT YOU ARE ABOUT TO BE TOLD 133

CHAPTER 25 THINKING THAT THE SKINNY RESIDENT WHO
KEEPS LOSING WEIGHT WILL BE OK   139

CHAPTER 26 DOING NOTHING ABOUT A STUDENT WHO
MAKES A SUICIDAL COMMENT   143

CHAPTER 27 ASSUMING THAT THE STUDENT WHO MAKES
SMALL CUTS ON DIFFERENT PARTS OF HER
BODY WANTS TO KILL HERSELF   149

CHAPTER 28 HELPING A RESIDENT, AND YOUR FLOOR,
SURVIVE A PANIC ATTACK   153

PART 6   THINGS THAT CAN SERIOUSLY
COMPROMISE YOUR ROLE   159

CHAPTER 29 BEING CARELESS ABOUT SPENDING
UNIVERSITY MONEY   161

CHAPTER 30 DECIDING WHAT TO DO BASED ON WHAT
EVERYONE ELSE DOES   165

CHAPTER 31 DATING A RESIDENT   169

CHAPTER 32 DRINKING ALCOHOL WITH UNDERAGE
RESIDENTS   173

CHAPTER 33 STAFF CONFLICT: DEALING WITH A SLACKING
STAFF MEMBER   179

CHAPTER 34 DEALING WITH PARENTS   183

PART 7   SAFETY AND SECURITY   189

CHAPTER 35 NOT GETTING EVERYONE OUT DURING A FIRE
ALARM   191

CHAPTER 36 TRYING TO HELP A RAPE SURVIVOR BUT
MAKING HER FEEL WORSE   195

CHAPTER 37 DEALING WITH SOMEONE WHO IS NOT A
STUDENT   201

CHAPTER 38 EXCUSING VIOLENT BEHAVIOR AS "JUST
BLOWING OFF STEAM"   207

CONCLUSION: REFLECTING ON THE IMPORTANCE OF THE
WORK WE DO   213

WHAT IS *YOUR* STORY?   219

ASK DR. JOHN   221

INDEX   223

About the Author

Dr. John D. Foubert received his BA in both Psychology and Sociology from the College of William and Mary, an MA in Psychology from the University of Richmond, and a PhD in College Student Personnel Administration from the University of Maryland at College Park.

Dr. Foubert began his career in residence life as an RA at the University of Richmond, where he was assigned to the most notoriously difficult floor in the wildest hall on campus at the time. His love for his job despite the most trying of circumstances (including an intentionally set fire, a flood down four flights of stairs, a 50-person fight, drug deals, thousands of dollars worth of vandalism, and a host of other interesting experiences) helped him determine that a career in student affairs was most definitely for him. Dr. Foubert finished his master's degree (despite the best efforts of his residents to distract him) and stayed at the University of Richmond, serving for two years as an Area Coordinator for Residence Life. He then felt led to return to the classroom, so he spent four years at the University of Maryland earning his PhD. While at Maryland, Dr. Foubert worked in the Office of Resident Life as Assistant Coordinator for Research, Coordinator for Staff Recruitment and Selection, and Special Assistant to the Director. Upon completion of his doctorate, he served four years as an

Assistant Dean of Students in charge of first-year residence life programs at the University of Virginia. He then changed his career path to become a faculty member at the College of William and Mary. At William and Mary, Dr. Foubert enjoys his days of teaching masters and doctoral students how to be student affairs administrators at higher education institutions and provides leadership to the national office of the nonprofit organization, "One in Four."

Dr. Foubert has published numerous articles on issues of direct relevance to college students. He has published research on predictors of student satisfaction in college and university residence halls, the experiences of students living in substance free housing, and cowrote a book chapter on assessment issues in residence life. He has also published articles on gender differences in the psychosocial development of college students, and the effects of student organization involvement on college student development. His other book, *The Men's Program*, is a highly influential work in the field of rape prevention on college campuses. Dr. Foubert has served as an editorial board member of the *Journal of College and University Student Housing* and has made approximately 100 professional keynote and other conference presentations to residence life and student affairs conferences. An award winning practitioner, scholar, and programmer, Dr. Foubert has been identified by the American College Personnel Association as an "Emerging Scholar" and was the runner-up for the National Dissertation of the Year Award from the National Association of Student Personnel Administrators. He lives in Williamsburg, Virginia, with his wife Susan, and his beagle-mixes, Ellie and Murry.

Preface

This book is written for you, the RA. Whether your title is "Resident Assistant," "Resident Advisor," "Dorm Counselor," or some other variation, this book is written by someone who has been through what you have or are about to go through in your role as a residence life staff member. Being an RA is without question one of the most challenging leadership experiences any student can have, and one of the most potentially rewarding adventures a person can experience.

While working as an RA, an Area Coordinator, an Assistant to the Director of Residence Life, and as an Assistant Dean of Students, I discovered that many RAs face similar experiences, and make common, avoidable mistakes. Over the years I have tried many different ways of sharing some of these mistakes with each new class of RAs I have encountered, in the hopes of preparing them for their work, and to help them avoid the common pitfalls of our work. This book is my best attempt to share these mistakes—many of which I have made myself—with as wide an audience as possible.

Each chapter of this book is written as a letter to you, a fellow RA. It is formatted as though it was written by someone who has served as an RA for one, two, or maybe three years. Each letter writer starts by telling you a little bit about the institution where the author works, what it is like to be a student there, where it is located—that sort of thing. Then, the writer shares his or her biggest mistake that was made during the previous year. After sharing the details of that mistake, the author talks about getting advice from a more seasoned person about how to tackle the problem in a different way. Next, the RA shares with you how the same problem, or a similar issue, was dealt with more effectively the next time. Each RA then summarizes the lessons learned from that experience, and wishes you the best of luck as you address similar issues. After concluding the letter, a list of provocative discussion questions follow. You might ask yourself these questions to solidify your learning in an active fashion. You might also discuss these questions in an RA class, with your staff during training, for an inservice, or at a staff meeting. Finally, some additional resources are suggested in case you would like more information about the issue addressed by that particular chapter.

The book is organized around several major themes, referred to as "Parts." Within each Part, there are several chapters that address that theme through letters written from the perspective of different RAs who had to address a particular issue related to the theme in that Part. For example, Part 5, "Helping Students With Psychological Difficulties," includes five chapters that provide you with provocative stories that should help you to better deal with students who ask you to keep their information confidential when doing so could cause harm, to help a student with an eating disorder, to help a suicidal student, to understand students who make cuts on their body without the intention to kill themselves, and to help a resident (and your floor) deal with someone having a panic attack.

Other major Parts in this book describe strategies for the basics of building community, how to build an inclusive community, how to provide support to residents, how to enforce policy fairly, how to avoid situations that can compromise your role, and how to keep your residents safe and secure. After these Parts, I offer some final reflections on the importance of the work that you do and challenge you to make the most of your experience on staff. After that, I ask you to share your own story with me. Who knows, it could end up in the second edition of this book someday. Finally, I offer my support to you during your experience on staff, and offer, if you would ever like another person's perspective, to give you a word of advice—Ask Dr. John—whenever you like.

I hope that you find this book to be a valuable tool as you face the many challenges that inevitably await you. Of course, it is important to remember that your best source of information about how to handle your role is your supervisor and the policies of your institution (and, of course, your local, state, and federal laws). This book is simply an attempt to offer additional perspectives that will provoke your thoughts about different situations you are likely to face, and moreover provoke spirited discussion with your fellow staff members. In short, this book is here to provoke discussion, not to provide answers.

As someone who has walked several miles in your shoes, I wish you all the best for the experience you are about to enter. If it is anything like my own, you will grow in ways you never imagined, make friends you never thought you'd be so fortunate to have, and will be able to look back on the experience as a defining point in your life for years to come. Go forth and make a difference!

John D. Foubert, PhD
Williamsburg, Virginia

Acknowledgments

The more I publish, the more I realize that writing is a group activity. Before Jay Whitney from Routledge suggested I author this book, I would have never thought of doing so. I am deeply in his debt for suggesting what I hope will be a helpful resource to RAs nationwide. Writing it has been an adventure. A special thanks to Jay for believing in me, and for knowing before I did that I could write this.

I am also grateful to Brandynne Cremedy for editing every bit of this book. Her perspective as a former RA and her terrific eye for clarity helped make this work much better than it otherwise would have been. I deeply appreciate Brandynne's straight-forward feedback and thorough comments on each chapter.

Thanks also to Greg Donahue for researching ideas for the many resources offered at the end of each chapter. Greg's ability to find helpful resources from a wide variety of areas substantially help round out the information provided herein—thanks Greg! Thanks also to Jerry Tatum for editorial assistance, to Paul Brockwell for contributing a scenario, and to David Shonka for trying.

I also thank the many students whom I have served as their RA, area coordinator, dean, supervisor, advisor, professor, and mentor. Many of their stories are reflected directly or indirectly in this book (with names and details changed to protect the innocent or guilty as the case may be). Without their inspiration, this book would not have been possible. Though his story is not reflected in this book, special thanks go to Mike Davis—the resident on my floor who always brightened my day when I was an RA.

I have been blessed with several professional mentors who have taken the time to guide me in my career path, and to whom I am deeply grateful. Special thanks, in chronological order, to Judy King, Mike Michaelson, Sharon DiFonzo, Scott Allison, Dick Mateer, Susan Komives, Marylu McEwen, Pat Mielke, Dick Stimpson, Bud Thomas, Larry Benedict, and David Leslie.

In closing, I offer heartfelt thanks to Susan, Ellie, and Murry for always supporting me in my work, and for putting up with me when I was distracted by my writing.

PART 1

BUILDING
COMMUNITY

The Basics

CHAPTER 1 BEING AWAY A LOT FROM THE FLOOR DURING
          THE FIRST WEEK OF SCHOOL

CHAPTER 2 WAITING UNTIL THE SECOND MONTH OF THE
          YEAR TO DO PROGRAMMING

CHAPTER 3 PLANNING AN EVENT WITH YOUR HALL
          COUNCIL AND DOING ALL THE WORK YOURSELF

CHAPTER 4 AVOIDING CONFLICT: SEEING IT AS HARMFUL
          TO COMMUNITY

CHAPTER 5 JUMPING INTO SERVICE WITHOUT LEARNING

CHAPTER 6 HELPING STUDENTS CHOOSE THEIR FRIENDS
          CAREFULLY: AVOIDING CULTS

Part 1 focuses on some of the basics of being an RA, much of which you will face during your first week on the job. In chapter 1, we learn from Elizabeth's experience about how to balance time with our friends and time spent with our residents as the year gets underway. David shows us in chapter 2 that procrastinating on programming is to be avoided at all costs. Despite the best intentions, Martha teaches us that even with lots of enthusiasm, no involvement equals no commitment on the part of our residents. Ellie shows us in chapter 4 that if we leave conflict alone, it will indeed get worse than if we confront it directly from the beginning. Megan then shows us how a sincere desire to help the less fortunate can alienate many people in the local community and lead to many missed chances to learn. Finally, John shows us how important it is to reach out to residents who may be making harmful choices in who they spend time with and how they make commitments to groups whose purpose is suspect. Together these stories should help you learn several valuable lessons as you get your year off to a great start.

BEING AWAY A LOT FROM THE FLOOR DURING THE FIRST WEEK OF SCHOOL

Dear Fellow RA,

Hi! My name is Elizabeth. This is my third year as an RA at Rural Mountain University. Here at RMU we have a strong campus community, mostly because there really isn't much to do nearby and we are in the middle of nowhere! Or so it seems anyway, but we make the most of it. We have a strong Greek system, numerous student organizations, and most everyone lives on campus. My first year on staff was a tough transition for me to make. I had a hall of first-year women, 50 of them. Can you believe it? Wow, that was a lot. Not only did I have a large number of residents, especially for an RA with first-year women only, I also got off to a bad start with them. I hope by hearing my story, you'll learn some lessons from my mistakes so that you don't fall into the same trap that I did.

The Situation

Things got off to a great start on opening day. Everyone was excited to be moving in, my residents seemed happy with the amenities of the hall (our hall is centrally located, we are one of the only air conditioned halls for first-year students on campus, and we have beautiful lounges on every floor). While I was checking in my residents, I was also so excited to see my sorority sisters and friends from my first year who stopped by the check-in table to say hi. There were so many parties that I got invited to attend that night. I have a hard time saying "no," so I ended up telling a lot of my friends that I'd see them out later that night once I finished with my residents.

The rest of opening day went well, I went to Orientation sessions with my residents, went to dinner with them, and had our first floor meeting. As soon as the meeting was over at 9 p.m., I was able to slip away and go out to parties. When I came back at 2 a.m., I checked my e-mail and I had 15 messages just from my residents, wondering where I was. Several had also IM'ed me and a few had sent me messages through facebook. I was so glad that they wanted to be in touch with me, but was a little overwhelmed (to say the least).

The next day I had promised to do lunch with my roommate from last year, so I got another RA to take my residents to lunch after the required Orientation session. I was able to make it to a few Orientation sessions with my residents that afternoon, and even walked them over to the dining hall for dinner before I went out with a group of my friends to catch up from the summer. Later that night I was taking a walk on campus with this guy I've been seeing, and I overheard a conversation that one of my residents, Sheila, was having with another resident of our building. Sheila was saying that her RA (me) "hated us" was "never around" and that they had to bother all the other RAs in the building every time they wanted something. Sheila said she felt totally abandoned and figured the year would just be awful. I was crushed.

Getting Some Advice

I went to see my Resident Director the next day to get her thoughts on what I should do. The first thing I discovered was that the training session that I missed during RA training was the one where they went over our responsibilities for being available to our residents. In that session, the staff talked about how important it is to be around for first-year students, particularly at the beginning of the year. I remembered back to my first-year, and recalled how much Sally, my RA, was around to answer questions and make everyone feel at home. As I thought about everything, I just felt like a total failure. My RD made sure I knew I wasn't a failure, but that I really needed to change what I was doing to better serve my residents. She also helped me to figure out some good strategies to maintain contact with my friends, but also to help them understand that I needed to be there for my residents more often. It is so hard to pass up social opportunities and time with friends who just wanted to get together, but in not being there for my residents, I was saying "no" to my residents by default—and they were being hurt by it.

A Second Chance

The next day I started staying on my floor with the door open, and walked room to room to touch base. My residents were a bit surprised to see so much of me, but after a couple days they realized that I was for real, and was interested in them as people. I found that once they saw me as more approachable and more available, that I was able to earn their confidence. They came to me with their problems, helped out with hall birthday parties, and we all formed strong relationships that actually still last until this day. In a few weeks I'm planning a hall reunion for all of us to get together.

Lessons Learned

The toughest lesson I had to learn as an RA was how to say "no" to my friends who wanted to go out. At first I didn't say "no" to anyone, but then discovered that by saying "yes" to everyone, I was leaving others behind—namely my residents, who really needed me most. So much of the job is easier when your residents get along with you well and see you as approachable, instead of just as "the RA." I also learned that my Resident Director was a great resource for ideas, support, and encouragement. I wasn't really sure what her role was when I started off the year, but now I rely on her for guidance and direction in my job, and in life in general. I learned that RDs (or Area Coordinators, Area Directors, or whatever they are called at your school) can be great resources and really enjoy helping students if you just approach them.

I hope that as your year starts off you will remember to invest your time on your floor from the very beginning. The rewards in having a much better year, and having close, lasting relationships with so many of them are wonderful. I hope you learn from my experience. Have a great year!

All my best,
Elizabeth

Discussion Questions

1. What are some of the different times when Elizabeth could have made different decisions to help her residents?
2. Why was it hard for her to say "no" to so many of her friends?
3. What effect did this have on her residents?
4. What are some strategies Elizabeth could have used to talk with her friends about her responsibilities?
5. What could have been some other consequences of Elizabeth not being around much of the first week of school?
6. What are some ways you can think of to make sure that you are available to your residents?
7. What are the most helpful things you learned from this scenario?
8. How will you act differently as an RA, based on this new knowledge?

Tips for Being Available to Residents

1. When you walk through your area, be sure to say hi to everyone who has their door open; it reminds them that you are around.
2. When you are in your room, keep the door open.
3. Post a schedule outside your door of times you are usually around; it can make residents stress out less if they know when to find you.
4. Explain to friends that you aren't choosing your residents over them; it is your job to be there for residents, so you need their patience!
5. Take advantage of short periods of time when you are between classes or about to go out to touch base with residents whom you have not seen recently.

2

Waiting Until the Second Month of the Year To Do Programming

Dear Fellow RA,

Hi. My name is David. I go to Wild West University. Honestly, we are anything but "wild" really, but WWU is a great place to go to school. Almost everyone lives on campus, and we win awards at the National Association for College and University Residence Halls all the time for our programming. We have a few student organizations on campus, but not too many. Most of the life on campus is within the residence halls. I was pretty intimidated when I came on staff, as several of the RAs in my building were experienced, and three had won national awards for their programs. Great—I thought—I was going to be the RA with the lowest turnouts at programs and they'd all be really boring.

The Situation

As with many things I don't want to do out of a fear that they won't go well, my initial strategy for programming was to procrastinate—I just put it off. I did everything I was supposed to do when my residents were moving in, got to know them, showed the first year and transfer students around. Basically, I did my job. Other floors in our building were having all of these great programs and getting everyone to come out. I told my residents I was planning something big and they'd find out what it was soon enough. They got interested in what it was, but increasingly got impatient with me. Unfortunately, I had no idea what "it" was, and just kept putting them off. They started hanging out on other people's floors a lot. They complained that we never did anything fun. Looking back on it, they were right.

In October, I decided to have my first program—an egg eating contest. I thought it would be a great idea. It had never been done before, so why not? Looking back on it, I have no idea what on earth I was thinking. Of course no one showed up, and I was left sitting there with 100 hard boiled eggs and no one to blame but myself. I was devastated.

Getting Some Advice

I went to talk with a friend of mine who was an RA last year and lived across campus from me. I told her how I was intimidated and everything, and I had no idea what to do with programming. She sat me down and we talked about the importance of starting early to help residents develop a routine that part of what they do is stuff with their hallmates. There wasn't much I could do about that at that point in the semester. But the rest, I could try. She suggested I get to know my residents better, figure out what they like to do, and make a program out of stuff they enjoy. So I gave it a try.

A Second Chance

I found out that lots of my residents were taking an astronomy class together. So, I called the astronomy department and asked if I could bring my residents over some night to use their high-powered telescope and look at the stars. I even convinced their astronomy professor to be there and show them the different stars he'd been talking about in class. They thought it was really cool, and by extension, so was I.

Lessons Learned

I guess it is a simple lesson that I learned in retrospect. Getting a late start with programming is a hard thing. Putting it off is a really bad idea. Every program doesn't have to be an award winner. We just need to give residents a chance to get together and maybe learn something they might not otherwise learn in the classroom. Residence halls can be great places for students to learn things they would never otherwise encounter. We have such an opportunity to educate them. Now I love programming more than any other part of my job. It just took some practice, and some effort. I hope you learn from my experience. Have a great year!

God bless,
David

Discussion Questions

1. When you hear the word "programming" what is the first word that comes to mind?
2. Are you excited about, intimidated by, or not sure about programming?
3. What are some of your ideas about programming?
4. When is it important to start planning programs?
5. What are some good strategies for making programs successful?
6. What was the best program your RA did last year? What made it so good?
7. How can you effectively involve your residents in planning programs?
8. What are the most helpful things you learned from this scenario?
9. How will you act differently as an RA, based on this new knowledge?

Resources

Resident Assistant Link—Programming Ideas
http://www.studentaffairslink.com/residentassistantlink/content.asp?c=1
ResidentAssistant.com—Program Ideas
http://www.residentassistant.com/programming/index.htm
ResidentAssistant.org—Program Ideas
http://www.residentassistant.org/viewcat.aspx?viewcat=2
ResLife.net—Articles on Programming
http://www.reslife.net/html/pwithp.html

Tips for Doing Great Programs

1. Find out what interests your residents and design your programs around those interests.
2. Start programming early in the year so it becomes part of your residents' routines.
3. Start planning your programs well in advance of when they occur.
4. Pick a time for your programs based on when most of your residents are around your area anyway.
5. Be sure to evaluate your programs afterward so you can learn what to do differently next time!

3

Planning an Event with Your Hall Council and Doing All the Work Yourself

Dear Fellow RA,

Hi! My name is Martha. I just finished my first year as an RA. As I reflect upon the last year, it sure has been quite an experience! I attend Coastal Private University. Here at CPU, we are located on the beautiful gulf coast, with many residence halls, including mine, overlooking the shore. Lots of students come here because they instantly fall in love with the natural beauty that is on campus, and surrounds it. It really is breathtaking! Unfortunately, lots of students take advantage of the scenery when they should be in class, and not everyone graduates on time, and about one-third don't graduate at all, but they sure do make some great memories along the way.

Living here in Reiter Hall is great—we have a huge grill outside with lots of picnic tables and benches. Last year when I lived in Reiter, we had cookouts all the time. Some of my greatest memories from last year are from hanging out at cookouts and just enjoying my friends and the view, playing beach volleyball, staying up to watch the sunrise, making out under the stars, etc.

The Situation

As soon as the year started, I was so excited to have our first barbecue, I couldn't stand it! I volunteered to be the advisor for our hall council, and at the first meeting told them they needed to have a barbecue quickly! They took some convincing, but they went along with the idea after they heard me talk about how great it would be. Toward the end of their first meeting, I had them appoint a cookout committee, and I told them we'd meet the next day for lunch to plan it out. I thought they were excited about it, but I guess in retrospect they just weren't feeling it as much as I was.

Only two of the six committee members showed up for the planning lunch. Not being one to give up easily, I told them what we needed to do to organize the event, and assigned each of them tasks to do. Nancy was in charge of reserving the space and Sally was in charge of publicity. As for the four people not there, we still gave them jobs to do of course! Carol had to buy the food, Anne had to get the charcoal, Betsy was in charge of drinks, and Katie was in charge of setting up and cleaning up. I told Sally to be sure to tell the four who didn't make the meeting what their jobs were.

So have you ever had an experience where you felt like you had to do everything yourself? The cookout was a disaster. Nancy never reserved the space, so I had to beg the reservations office the day of the event to let us have the space. Sally never publicized the event, so I had to IM everyone at the last minute. Carol bought the food, but forgot to get a receipt. Anne didn't buy any charcoal at all and just bailed on us. Betsy bought a bunch of beer even though it was a hall program and most students were under 21. And Katie never showed to set up, let alone clean up. We ended up having to cancel the event a few minutes after the starting time once I realized we had no charcoal and so few people were there. The people who did show up were annoyed because they planned on that being their dinner and they hadn't eaten, and it was too late to go to the dining hall. I was stuck with all this uncooked food that we couldn't get reimbursed for because we had no receipt, and it wasn't used at the program! I had a major meltdown.

Getting Some Advice

My Area Director saw me crying in the cookout area, so she came out of her apartment to see what was wrong. I explained everything about how I had it all organized and planned but then it all fell apart. She asked me how I went about planning the event, how much the residents were involved in making decisions, how much they felt ownership over those decisions and what not. During the course of our conversation, my eyes opened a lot about how, and how not, to plan an event with hall council. I realized that I tried to do all the work myself and boss everyone around, instead of involving them from step one. Even when I delegated tasks, it was for my way of getting things done; not necessarily theirs. I had created my own disaster, and now it was time to learn from it and move on.

A Second Chance

During the next hall council meeting, I apologized for trying to run things too much. They all breathed a big sigh of relief—it was like a huge burden had been lifted. We had a really deep conversation about how they thought I didn't care about their ideas, and that they really valued my help but didn't want to be told what to do. It was great to air everything out. By the end of the meeting, we had planned a fall semi-formal dance that everyone was super excited about—I was excited too because they were happy to have me help.

Lessons Learned

I learned so many lessons I will never forget from this experience. I learned a phrase I now live by: no involvement equals no commitment. I learned the hard way that when you work with hall council, they are not your employees; they are volunteers. They need to buy into an idea, even think it is theirs, or there won't be energy behind it. In my rush to get them to do things my way, I just steamrolled right over them, and they had no investment in the process. I know that in your RA experience, you'll probably learn different kinds of lessons than I did. By hearing about my experience, I'm sure you won't repeat my mistakes! Have a great year on staff.

Fondly,
Martha

Discussion Questions

1. At what points could Martha have used a more effective style of advising hall council to plan an event?
2. How is dictating different from supervising?
3. How is supervising different from advising?
4. What are some techniques you've seen in advisors you've worked with that have worked really well?
5. Why do you think they worked well—what about the group or situation made them effective?
6. When should an RA step in and do the work for hall council?
7. When is it OK to let a program fail?
8. What are the most helpful things you learned from this scenario?
9. How will you act differently as an RA, based on this new knowledge?

Resources

National Clearinghouse for Leadership Programs
http://www.nclp.umd.edu/
Leadership Web site with tips and quizzes
http://www.leadersdirect.com/
Leadership site with articles
http://www.emergingleader.com/
Student Leader, the magazine of the ASGA
http://www.asgaonline.com/studentleader/

Tips on Working with Hall Council

1. Remember that they are volunteers who need guidance and motivation!
2. Try not to shoot down their ideas too quickly. A crazy idea, redirected, can lead to a great event!
3. If their energy is flowing and they aren't talking about doing anything against policy or illegal, step back and let them run with it!

4. Mention some ideas to individual members before the meeting and let them take the credit.
5. Have them regularly evaluate their programs at the meeting following each event, so that they are used to giving and receiving feedback to make their efforts more effective.

4

AVOIDING CONFLICT

Seeing It as Harmful to Community

Dear Fellow RA,

Hey! My name is Ellie. I'm so excited to be sharing a lesson I learned the hard way with y'all. I'm a head resident this year in the hall where I've been an RA for three years now. I attend "Southern State University"—one of the biggest schools in the South, with lots of special traditions and great athletic teams. Go Beagles, you gotta dig 'em!

So, I grew up in the South. My whole family lived by my grand-momma's creed, "If you don't have anything nice to say, don't say anything at all." While it had its strong points, it meant that we didn't really deal with conflict very well. Thus, I didn't learn to deal with it at all, and it blew up in my face my first year on staff in a big way, a really big way.

The Situation

I was so excited for opening day I didn't sleep a wink all night. I stayed up until 5 a.m. decorating my hall, and tried to take a power nap before opening, but it just didn't happen. So anyway, move in went just great, all the women on my hall got along instantly, stayed together as a group throughout orientation week, ate meals together, just what I had hoped. Once classes started, a lot of them had the same courses, so they'd walk to class together and go to lunch; we even had our own table we always went to in the dining hall for dinner. It was simply blissful!

On the weekends, about half of the hall went out to parties, and the other half of them hung out on the floor, went to see a movie, or studied. One Saturday morning I went into the bathroom to take a shower, and I noticed that things were kind of tense between a few of my residents. Katie and Molly, two of the most popular women on the floor, were not talking back and forth like they usually did. I just figured that they were in a bad mood or something; no big deal. Once I got in the shower, I heard one of them say that "b" word that rhymes with "witch" and leave the bathroom. I wasn't sure if I misheard it, if they were talking about me, or if one was saying something to the other. So, I just ignored it.

The rest of the day, things were weird. Usually, everyone on my hall kept their doors open and talked in the hallways to each other. That day, all the doors were closed most of the time, and small groups of women would be talking in each other's rooms real quiet. Every once in awhile I heard a door slam shut. Yikes! I kind of thought something was up, but didn't want to deal with it so I called my friend Sarah Jane and we went out to a movie that night so I could get away from all that tension and unpleasantness.

What I thought would just blow over, didn't. Things stayed tense on my hall all week. The next weekend it got worse. I woke up one morning to Katie and Molly screaming at each other saying all kinds of words I don't like to hear, and in grammatically correct combinations that I never thought possible. It is amazing how creative women can be with their combinations of cuss words. I just couldn't believe they were being so rude. As I sat in my room trying to ignore them, my residents started IM'ing me saying, "Can't you hear that?" "Tell them to shut up!" I couldn't stand it any longer so I turned my computer off, turned my fan on for background noise, and took a nap.

The tension got worse and worse all week, people on the hall took sides, and things on the floor were never the same. It turns out that Katie and Molly got into a disagreement initially over what party to attend. Katie wanted to go to a party with members of the soccer team, and Molly wanted to go to a Kappa Epsilon Gamma party. Well, Molly's way won out, Katie started dancing with a guy Molly was interested in, and it went downhill from there. Katie hooked up with the guy that Molly was interested in and, the next week, Molly did the same thing to Katie.

Getting Some Advice

In my end of the semester evaluation, my Resident Director asked me why I seemed to be so happy with my hall during the first half of the semester and seemed down about them during the second half. I broke down and told her everything that happened with Katie, Molly, the slamming doors, the situation that basically just got out of hand. Right now, it seems so ridiculous, but then it seemed like the biggest deal in the world. It took awhile, but my RD was able to show me how, when managed delicately, conflict can actually help a hall grow together. She taught me how to turn a conflict into a learning experience about getting along with others. After all, our residents will be living and interacting with lots of people in the future—they might as well learn now about how to manage the inevitable conflicts that arise.

A Second Chance

In January when everyone came back, I spoke with Katie and Molly separately, then together. At our first hall meeting, I acknowledged that things had been tense last fall, and that I was hoping that things would be better this semester. We worked out a way to deal with conflict on the floor, and Katie and Molly let everyone know they had resolved their differences and were friends again. Though things were never as tight as they were during the first semester, they sure were a lot better than they had been!

Lessons Learned

I learned so much from my experience as an RA, particularly from resolving the Katie and Molly conflict. First, I came to terms with the fact that conflict is inevitable. It is just going to happen! Second, the "don't say anything at all" method is bound to make things worse. Third, when conflict occurs, it is best to acknowledge it, resolve it, and move on. I sure will approach things that way in the future! I hope when you have residents who have a conflict that you will handle it a lot better than I did. Acknowledge the conflict, talk it through, and move on. Have a great year!

Affectionately,
Ellie

Discussion Questions

1. Looking back on this case, when are times when Ellie had the chance to say something but didn't?
2. When do you think it would have been best for Ellie to say something?
3. Who should she have talked to, and what should she have said?
4. Why can it be tempting to avoid conflict?
5. What are the possible results of avoiding conflict?
6. What are some general principles for dealing with conflict that are effective?
7. How do you personally deal with conflict?
8. In what ways can you improve in dealing with conflict?
9. What are the most helpful things you learned from this scenario?
10. How will you act differently as an RA, based on this new knowledge?

Resources

Campus Conflict Information
http://www.campus-adr.org/Student_Center/tips_student.html
The Conflict Resolution Information Source
http://www.crinfo.org/
Association for Conflict Resolution
http://www.acrnet.org/
Conflict Resolution through Mediation
http://www.reslife.net/html/tools_1004a.html

Tips on Dealing with Conflict

1. Figure out your own attitudes about conflict and figure out how best to keep them in check when conflict arises.
2. Look for the ways to channel conflict to strengthen community.
3. When things get tense, mention verbally that things seem tense to help diffuse the situation.
4. Most of the time if you can say what it seems everyone is thinking, it can help focus the discussion.
5. Center your efforts on identifying potential solutions, but don't tell people how they should resolve it. They need to own their plan to resolve the conflict.

5

JUMPING INTO SERVICE WITHOUT LEARNING

Dear Fellow RA,

Hi! My name is Megan. I just finished my second year as an RA at Wealthy University. WU is a small private school in New England with rich tradition and high tuition. Most of the students who come here come from families that can afford to pay their full tuition bill without any financial aid. Let's just say that there isn't much poverty here. There are rich kids and ridiculously rich kids.

Both of my years on staff were great; but my first year I really learned a lot, and now realize I had a lot to learn! Back in my first year on staff, I just loved the women on my floor. We all bonded really quickly and had great times all year long. Sorority rush was a tough time, of course, but lots of them got in where they wanted and those who didn't connected to other organizations they really liked—everyone was happy. During the spring semester, we decided to do a community service project together. What a great idea to help out those less fortunate, or so I thought. Little did I know that it would not go too well; if I had done a little more planning, it would have been so much more worthwhile for everyone involved in the activity. So here's what happened.

The Issue

Becky, one of the most involved women on my hall, came to me after winter break and said she thought we should all get together and do a service project for our local community to help the less fortunate in the inner city near our campus. I told her it was a great idea and to bring it up at the next hall meeting. She did, and everyone liked the idea. Another resident, Amanda, said she had read an article that week about a lot of young kids in a neighborhood who kept getting into drugs and gangs because they had nothing else to do. We all decided that we would reach out to underprivileged children and play with them for an afternoon. Everyone loved the idea.

We got a phone book, and started calling people who lived in the neighborhood we wanted to help. We told them we were from Wealthy University and were planning a "Play Day" for underprivileged children in their neighborhood. That was our first mistake. A lot of parents reacted funny when we said "underprivileged children." We weren't real sure at the time why, after all, we just wanted to help. As it turns out, they found it condescending for us to label their children "underprivileged"—especially because they were working so hard as parents to care for their children.

After having lots of people hang up on us, we finally got a small group of kids to come to a local park to play. About 15 of us went over. Only six kids came; we were kind of bummed about not having more kids, but we did the best we could. We played with them on the swings, the slide, and even organized a game of dodge ball. Their mothers sat together at a nearby picnic table; I think they were intimidated to talk to us, or maybe we were to them, I'm not really sure to be honest.

At the end of the afternoon, the kids asked us when we were having another play day. We told them it was our one community service project of the year, so we weren't planning another one. They looked a little disappointed; which was kind of a complement to us; they actually wanted to see us again! But, it was near the end of the semester, and that was all we could do. After that, we all went back to campus and went back to our normal routines. I couldn't help but think that we could have done a better job, but I wasn't sure what else we could have done. So, I decided to go talk with Dr. Jesstell, the Director of Service Learning in our Student Activities office. Wow, did I learn a lot then.

Getting Some Advice

We really missed the chance to make our experience, and that of those we were trying to serve, much more meaningful. Dr. Jesstell taught me that with a little more planning, and a little more time, there is so much more everyone could have gotten out of our Play Day. First, he taught me the difference between "community service" and "service learning." I thought they were the same thing. But no! Community service can be almost any activity where people are helping others in need. But service learning has two key added components—reciprocity and reflection. Reciprocity, in this context, means that those being served control the service provided. In other words, the needs of the community, as determined by its members, define what the service tasks will be. As part of service learning, reciprocity also means that we do things *with* others rather than for them. In addition, we can look at the experience as something we can grow from, not just help others through. Reflection, the other important concept, helps us all learn more from our experience. What did we just do? Why did we do it? How were we affected by it? How were the kids affected? How were the parents affected? Why is it that we live in a society where some people like us are advantaged, and others are not?

A Second Try

So this year, I followed Dr. Jesstell's advice. In September, I met with Dr. Jesstell to get his ideas on different projects where there was a need. Then, I contacted the director of the local rape crisis center to get an understanding of their needs, and how the women on my floor could fit into that. We found out that lots of women come there with their kids who really need a friendly person with whom to play. Some of the women just like to talk to someone when they are not talking with their counselor. My residents loved the idea, and we decided to go every Friday afternoon of the school year to play with the kids and talk with the moms. We learned so much from their experiences, and even learned a few lessons about what it feels like to be sexually assaulted. Several women on the floor were so inspired that they started a peer education group on campus, and invited some of the women from the center to talk with students about their experiences. We also worked with a sociology professor, who organized an independent study class for us to write reflection papers about our experiences. It was so much better the second time around!

Lessons Learned

So, as you can tell by now, planning a service learning project (not just community service) is tough but worthwhile. If you want to do something like I did, here's what I suggest. First, meet with someone on your campus who has experience with service learning. It could be someone in your Student Activities office, Dean of Students office, College of Arts and Sciences, or a faculty member. Then, contact someone in the community to get an understanding of their needs, and how your residents could fit into those needs. Seek to do a project where you work with members of the community to do something together, rather than just a haphazard activity. Finally, ask a faculty or staff member to meet with you after your project to help your residents make the connection between what they did, what they learned from it, and how you can apply what they learned to their understanding of society. I hope you can learn from my experience. Good luck!

Cheers,
Megan

Discussion Questions

1. What are some areas in which it sounds like Megan was successful during her first year as an RA?
2. What were some of her mistakes when approaching the project she did with her residents in April?
3. Aside from the approach that she took in her "second try" what are some other more promising approaches she could have taken?
4. What approach do you think is best for undertaking a service learning project?
5. Do you think it is worthwhile to extend community service into service learning?

6. What are some things you might do in the community near campus to put a project together? Who would you contact? Where?

8. What are the most helpful things you learned from this scenario?

9. How will you act differently as an RA, based on this new knowledge?

Resources

Books:

Jacoby, B. (2003) *Building Partnerships for Service Learning.* San Francisco: Jossey Bass.

Eyler, J. & Giles, D. E. (1999). *Where's the Learning in Service Learning?* San Francisco: Jossey-Bass.

Web sites:

National Service-Learning Clearinghouse
http://www.servicelearning.org/hehome/index.php
Campus Compact—Service Learning Resources
http://www.compact.org/resource/SLres-print_web.html
Big Dummy's Guide to Service Learning
http://www.fiu.edu/~time4chg/Library/bigdummy.html
Service Learning Resource Kit
http://www.edb.utexas.edu/servicelearning/resource.html

Tips for Making the Most of Service Learning Experiences

1. Meet with a faculty member or administrator as you plan your program to help identify ways to make it into a service learning experience.

2. Don't assume your residents will make the learning connections on their own; help them structure an experience to make community service into a learning experience.

3. Find out what your residents are learning in their classes, and organize a service learning experience around what they are already learning.

4. Look at the mission statement for your institution and get ideas for the types of service that your institution prizes.

5. Read a local newspaper to figure out the needs in your local community that you and your residents might be able to help with and learn from!

6

HELPING STUDENTS CHOOSE THEIR FRIENDS CAREFULLY

Avoiding Cults

Dear Fellow RA,

My name is John. I come from a small town in Tennessee. I decided to go to school out of state, unlike most of my friends. I'm a student at Big State University; this is my third year as an RA. Here at BSU, we have about 30,000 students. Most of the life around here is on campus, and close by. We are located in a relatively small town in an area far away from a big city. Back where I grew up, just about everyone went to church on Sunday. I started out going to the church across the street from my residence hall when I was a first-year student. Right now I'm taking a break from organized religion while I figure things out on my own. I'll probably return to it some day; right now, it's just not for me. Lots of people explore different religious beliefs here at BSU. There are also lots of groups out there to help people explore them. Most of those groups are pretty decent, but last year I found out that not all of them have the best interests of others in mind.

The Situation

It was my second year as an RA. I thought I had seen everything. The other RAs in my building looked up to me for advice, for help with policy enforcement, for thoughts about how to do their first program and that kind of stuff. My residents were pretty cool too. Not like the great guys I had the year before, but nothing could really live up to that I guess. There was this one guy on the floor, Tommy, who nobody really talked with much. He kept to himself and didn't get in anyone's way. I stopped by his room once or twice during the first week. He didn't seem to be interested in anything I had to say. Later, his roommate Sunil told me that Tommy found me annoying. No big deal; I left him alone.

Around October, I noticed that Tommy wasn't around the floor much anymore. The only time I'd see him would be sitting out in front of our residence hall. Most of the time when Tommy was outside of our residence hall he would be alone, except when a few people from off campus would stop to talk with him. Tommy didn't really have many friends; that was obvious. By November, I realized I hadn't seen him in three weeks. Sunil said he went to live in a house off campus, saying that was the only place he could be accepted. His parents called looking for him and said they didn't know where he was. I thought it was odd, but no big deal. I was wrong.

My RD called me in and asked if I knew much about Tommy. "Not much," I told her. She then told me that Tommy had joined a cult. A cult? That was just plain weird, I thought. My RD explained that it was a serious situation. Tommy had been recruited outside my residence hall by three cult members who were working together, looking for lonely students who sought out easy answers to life's problems. Tommy was their perfect mark. They offered him friends, a place where he'd be accepted, and all the easy answers he wanted. They lured him in by talking about how their leader would solve all of his problems. I know this sounds crazy, but they actually told him that he'd be put on a list of 66 people to be saved (one for every book in the Bible) if he'd just move into their house, get a job, give all his money to them, and follow all of their rules. It turns out, this kind of thing was more common than we thought.

Getting Some Advice

We asked a religion professor who specialized in fringe groups to come in and talk with our staff about cults. The biggest thing we learned is that you can't tell a cult by its religious beliefs. Rather, cults are distinguished mostly by how they recruit and retain members. While no one thing necessarily makes a group a cult, Professor Josephson explained that they tend to be organizations that require absolute obedience to a charismatic group leader, separation from other family and friends, a substantial amount of money and required service, relocation to cult sponsored housing, and pressure to quit school or a job to serve them. According to an article he read (referenced below) there are several characteristics of a group that make it more likely to be considered a cult. These characteristics include a prohibition on talking with outsiders who won't convert, deception about the group's nature and purpose, and focused recruitment during stressful times of a college semester.

A Second Try

Tommy ended up dropping out of school. In retrospect, I wish I had been more assertive about helping him get involved on campus. I also wish I knew more about the different religious groups on campus, and around town, so I could have given my residents the best advice possible. This year I told all my guys about Tommy's experience (of course I didn't give them his name). The Director of Residence Life also asked me to speak about cults during RA training, so that other staff members know a little bit about what they are, and are not. Hopefully by learning more about these groups, residents can make informed choices about who to associate with and who they want to avoid.

Lessons Learned

I'd have to say I learned a lot from being an RA, and never thought the big lesson I'd learn is the importance of reaching out to students who don't appear to want help from an RA. Lots of first-year students are just plain scared when they get to college. Some don't know how to fit in. Some seek easy answers to life's problems, and are susceptible to groups who don't have their best interests in mind. There are lots of great religious groups out there—but some groups will target students in unhealthy ways and get them to do things that are dangerous—cutting off ties with family, dropping out of school, etc. There really are cults out there—it isn't just something that happened years ago. Many are based near college campuses. Part of our responsibility is to educate our residents so that they make good decisions, and work to help them fit into life on campus in a way they find meaningful. It is a great challenge, but a worthy cause. Good luck with your year on staff! I hope you learned something from my experience. Have a great year!

Thanks,

John

Discussion Questions

1. What distinguishes a cult from other groups?
2. Do you think there are students on our campus who would be susceptible to recruitment by a cult?
3. What kind of student?
4. What kinds of things should we tell our residents about these different groups?
5. If we suspect that one of our residents is being recruited by a cult, where do we draw the line between warning them of the potential dangers and making decisions for them?
6. How might our own religious beliefs affect our attitudes toward cults?
7. What are the most helpful things you learned from this scenario?
8. How will you act differently as an RA, based on this new knowledge?

Resources

Cults on campus: Perspectives from the literature
http://jdfoub.people.wm.edu/Foubert96.pdf

Helping Residents Avoid Cults

1. Tell your residents that cults really do exist and that college students are often their prey.
2. Be very careful about telling residents that a particular group is a cult. Instead, share with them what characteristics tend to be in cult groups and help them evaluate things for themselves.
3. Avoid making your residents paranoid that every group on and off campus might be a cult.
4. Help your residents understand that you can't tell a cult by its theology, only by its recruitment and retention techniques.
5. Encourage residents to explore their spiritual development.

PART 2

BUILDING AN INCLUSIVE COMMUNITY

CHAPTER 7   ASSUMING STUDENTS IN A RACIAL MINORITY
            DON'T WANT TO BE INCLUDED IN HALL ACTIVITIES

CHAPTER 8   TRYING TO HELP A STUDENT OF A DIFFERENT
            RACE AND MAKING THINGS WORSE

CHAPTER 9   IGNORING RACIST COMMENTS

CHAPTER 10 A CASE OF RELIGIOUS DISCRIMINATION

CHAPTER 11 THE FACEBOOK NIGHTMARE

The chapters in Part 2 get deeper into the intricacies of leading your community. A major theme of these chapters relates to how we need to make our areas good places for everyone to live, not just members of a privileged majority. The chapters also help us understand some of the challenges in dealing with issues like race, religion, and online communities. In chapter 7, we learn from Jill's experience about how RAs who have not before experienced difference can struggle to connect with people of a different race. Garrett's experience shows us that making faulty assumptions can really alienate a resident. Brian's experience teaches us the importance of confronting racist comments and making it clear that they are not acceptable from the beginning, instead of allowing them to fester. The dynamics on Joe's floor shows how world events can change the dynamic quickly among residents, and lead to the alienation of people from religious groups that face marginalization at any given point in time. And then there is JoAnn's floor, which got caught up in a quagmire of miscommunication and misunderstanding and perhaps some misjudgment too with an online social network. By thinking through these finer points of community building before you even begin your service on staff, you can be ready to face these challenges square on!

7

ASSUMING STUDENTS IN A RACIAL MINORITY DON'T WANT TO PARTICIPATE IN HALL ACTIVITIES

Dear Fellow RA,

Hi. My name is Jill. I grew up in a rural community in the South and I attend Southern Heritage University. SHU is a large state school, and is the place where most of the politicians and business leaders in our state went to get their college degrees. Our state has strong racial divisions. SHU was all White until 1971 when Black students, the only other racial group in the state with more than 2% of the population, were first admitted. Even though we've been integrated for awhile, there are still racial divisions here. There are "White" organizations and "Black" organizations. There are "White" parties and "Black" parties. About the only place there is racial mixing is in the classroom and in the residence halls. I have to admit, having a racially mixed floor was an adjustment for me. For whatever reason, during my first year of college I didn't interact much with the few Black students in my building; and they were the first Black students with whom I had ever even gone to school.

The Situation

So on to the situation. I arrived for RA training along with my whole family. Moving my stuff into the dorm is quite a project. I have a very particular way I like things, and I expect to have as many of the comforts of home as possible. My oldest brother, Tyler, calls me a princess. I plead guilty as charged. My mom is an interior decorator, so she spends a lot of time setting up my room at the beginning of every year. My dad and my brothers provide the muscle to move in my stereo, DVD player, and, of course, my wardrobe; it could make a queen jealous.

A couple days into RA training, Shantay, Jobila, and Michelle moved in. SHU started an orientation program a few years ago just for the Black students to help them get adjusted to the university before other students move in, so they were here to participate in that program. I knew they were coming in early, so I had their door tags done and on their doors before they arrived. That day after RA training was over, I stopped by each of their rooms to welcome them to SHU. They were a little nervous but polite, and seemed to be getting their rooms set up OK. They spent the next few days in their orientation program while I finished RA training. When everyone else arrived, Shantay, Jobila, and Michelle were mostly out of the hall either doing day-trips with other Black students, or hanging out in other parts of campus. I asked them one day to go with us to an Orientation event, and they said they already went through Orientation and didn't need to go. Although I explained that this was a session they had not had, they didn't seem interested, so I just let it drop. I got the message that they weren't really interested in interacting with their fellow residents, so I didn't bother trying anymore. This ended up being a mistake. There was no big "blow up" or anything, but as time went on, I realized that the racial divide on campus was being repeated on my floor, and there was something that didn't really sit well with me about that.

Getting Some Advice

I decided to go talk with Dr. Jones, my psychology professor, after class one day about the situation. She also teaches a course on the psychology of race and gender, so I figured she might have some ideas to offer. I explained how the Black students on my floor weren't mixing with the White students and I didn't know what to do. Let's just say we had a really long conversation about it. One of the things Dr. Jones brought to my attention was how my own attitude might have affected

Shantay, Jobila, and Michelle and how they felt about being part of the floor community. At first, I thought Dr. Jones was making me out to be some kind of racist pig, but I realized that with my upbringing, there were some expectations and stereotypes I had in my head that I relied on unconsciously that were affecting my role as an RA. I realized that I thought Black students preferred to not interact with others, that they would rather just keep to themselves, and that they were basically unfriendly and stand-offish people. It took me awhile to admit that, but once I realized how I needed to rethink my perceptions, I thought about how I could do my job differently. Of course, the last thing I wanted to do was to be a pain in the butt and insist that Shantay, Jobila, and Michelle be best friends with everyone on the floor and hang out with everyone all the time. Students, regardless of race, should make their own decisions about who to hang with and how to spend their down time. However, as an RA, I realized I had a unique role to play in setting norms for my community. When I asked people on the floor to go to dinner, did everyone feel welcome to come? Did I invite everyone or did I skip over some people? When I was planning a program for the floor, did I include ideas from different people on the floor, or just from the people who usually came to what I did. I realized that I hadn't really reached out to Shantay, Jobila, and Jennifer and find out how they liked to spend time, how they liked to relax.

A Second Chance

After talking with Dr. Jones, I hung out in Jobila's room one day. She looked a little surprised to see me, but got over that after awhile. I discovered that she was a yoga instructor. I asked if she'd give a yoga lesson as a hall program, and she agreed. Over half the floor came out for the event, and it was a great opportunity for people to get to know each other better. It was far from the magic solution to break down the racial divide on my hall, but it was a step in the right direction. Several of the women on the floor started taking Jobila's yoga class in the Rec Center, so that was one more way that my residents mingled outside the hall.

Lessons Learned

I can't say that we are a model floor of racial harmony. Honestly, that is going to take some time on my floor, and moreover at my university. But I can say that I learned more about how I as an RA can work to build a more inclusive community, and to rethink my assumptions and stereotypes. I never expected that this would be the biggest lesson I'd learn all year, but it was. I'm still learning, of course, and I hope I always will be. More than anything, I hope that you learn from my experience. Have a great year!

Sincerely,
Jill

Discussion Questions

1. Why might Jill have assumed that Shantay, Jobila, and Jennifer didn't want to participate in floor activities?
2. What role might Jill's background have played in coming to this conclusion?
3. What stereotypes might Jill have maintained about African Americans that might have supported this conclusion?
4. What strategies could Jill have used from the beginning to promote a community that was inclusive of people from all races?
5. What is the appropriate line for the RA to draw between encouraging integrated floor activities and respecting people's desires and comfort zones?
6. What are some specific things Jill could have done differently in this scenario?
7. Do you think there is a racial divide on your campus? Why or why not?
8. What can RAs do to promote a more racially inclusive community on your campus?
9. What are the most helpful things you learned from this scenario?
10. How will you act differently as an RA, based on this new knowledge?

Resources

ResLife.net—Building positive communities
http://www.reslife.net/html/tools_0603a.html
Diversity Web—AAC&U
http://www.diversityweb.org/index.cfm
Developing A Diversity Mindset: The Ripple Effect
http://www.reslife.net/html/tools_1002a.html
National Coalition Building Institute
http://www.ncbi.org/

Tips on Crossing Racial Divides

1. Don't assume that a member of a race different from your own is just like every other member of that race you have met before.
2. Approach people different from you with a desire to learn their needs from them, not based on your presuppositions.
3. Especially if you are working with students different from you whom you don't have much experience with, be patient; it may take you a while to learn how best to relate most effectively to people different from you.
4. Have an open dialogue with people different from you and ask questions instead of assuming you know.
5. Keep trying; working on racial issues isn't easy no matter what your background.

8

TRYING TO HELP A STUDENT OF A DIFFERENT RACE AND MAKING THINGS WORSE

Dear Fellow RA,

My name is Garrett Callahan, and I'm an RA at Oldham University. Oldham University is a mid-sized university in a midwestern state. We have a very proud tradition of athletic dominance in our conference, and we have a particularly strong School of Engineering. About half of the students at OU come from within the state, about one-third from contiguous states, and the rest from across the country.

The biggest mistake I made as an RA was assuming that an African American student on my floor was "anti-white" because of a big change I saw in his attitude during the middle of the year. Let me explain. I come from a small town in North Dakota. The first time I ever met someone who wasn't White was when I came to college. I didn't know a lot about people different from me. I found it exciting to meet new people, but a little intimidating when I saw groups of people clustering together by race and that sort of stuff. Anyway, I became an RA during my sophomore year and had 20 great guys on my floor. One of them, Andre, was an African-American guy from a big city. He was the only guy on the floor who wasn't White. Not a big deal, I figured, as most guys on the hall seemed nice to him. He even had dinner with us a couple times a week when we went over to the dining hall. Andre was kind of quiet but seemed to be doing well. He seemed to enjoy his classes and hung out with several different groups of friends in the evenings and on the weekends.

The Situation

In November, Andre came home one afternoon and was just really angry and really loud. He stormed back into his room, got on his cell phone, and was yelling into it saying the "n" word, saying how he hated this place; he just went on and on forever. He was so loud that it seemed like the whole building was vibrating. One of the guys on the floor who had been taking a nap came and complained to me that Andre woke him up. I figured that Andre was just blowing off some steam; no big deal. The next week, Andre started eating exclusively at one of the "black tables" in the dining hall. He joined the "Black Student Alliance" and changed his major to African-American Studies. He didn't hang out on the floor anymore, and when he did, it was with his friends from the BSA who came by to see him. Most of the guys on the floor stopped talking to him.

I decided to have a talk with Andre. I asked him to come to my room and chat. This is where I made my big mistake. Well, actually, I made several big mistakes all in one sitting. I'm talented that way. I told Andre that the guys on the floor really liked him, but that they were talking about how he'd been turning all "anti-white" and stuff. I let him know how annoyed one of the guys was with him when he was yelling that time on his cell phone. Then, I told him how great it was at Oldham University for us to meet people different from ourselves, and that by self-segregating in the dining hall and in student organizations that he was really missing out on what OU had to offer. Finally, I said that I hoped to see him start eating with the floor again in the dining hall so that we could show everyone how tight we all are as a floor. Andre sat there and just listened. When I was through, he asked, "Are you finished?" I said, "Yes," and he left.

Getting Some Advice

Nothing really changed, and I couldn't understand why. I decided to go talk with Dr. Gray, my introductory psychology professor, about it. She also taught in the African-American Studies Department, so I figured she might have some insight that could be helpful to me in this situation. She listened to everything I said, smiled, sighed, and then opened my eyes to a lot of things I did not understand before.

The first piece of advice she gave me was that in the future, I should ask students questions about their situation, rather than just jumping to conclusions about it. For example, Andre's behavior that afternoon when he came back so angry could easily have been due to his experiencing an incident of racism. The fact that he used the "n" word as he was yelling about it only reinforced that point. Andre may very well have been repeating a word that was spoken to him. His eating with other people of his race and choosing to study issues of race is a common reaction to having experienced an incident of racism. Dr. Gray suggested I go back and ask Andre if I could have another conversation with him. I took her advice.

A Second Try

The next day, I talked with Andre. This time, I asked questions and listened to his responses. It turns out, Andre answered a question incorrectly in class and his professor said to him "Next time, do the reading." A few guys sitting behind him then laughed and used the "n" word in a disparaging way toward him. It turns out, Andre had done the reading, he just didn't get the point the professor was making. When ostracized by his classmates, he was embarrassed, hurt, and angry. He got the feeling that the only ones who could really understand his experience were people of his own race, so, he began spending more time with African Americans and less time with his floor and other White people. Andre explained to me that he just needed some time to figure out what his race meant to him, and how he could deal with the pressures of being in such a small racial minority on campus. Andre explained that the incident made him question a lot of the motives of White people, whether they were nice or not, and he just needed to explore his racial identity. He also told me that when he was eating with other students of his race in the cafeteria, it had nothing to do with segregation. He taught me that segregation was not a choice in the United States, it was a legal way to keep people of different races in separate schools and public places. He explained to me that sometimes African-American students self-select to eat together for social support, friendship, and to avoid having to feel like they are being looked at or judged on the basis of their race. He also noted that lots of White students eat together too, but no one really questions that.

After talking with him—and listening this time—I realized that there was nothing wrong with the decisions Andre was making about who to hang out with, what to study, and who to eat with in the dining hall. I realized that I had no idea what it felt like to be in such a small minority on campus, particularly one that had been historically oppressed, and that I had a lot to learn from his experience. I also realized that I should always begin a conversation by asking questions instead of jumping to conclusions. I learned a lot about issues of race through this whole situation. I know I'll handle such situations differently in my next year as an RA. Hopefully by reading about my experience, you will handle such situations differently as well.

Lessons Learned

I learned so many lessons from this experience. First, when talking with a resident about a concern you have, always begin by asking questions to figure out where he or she is coming from. Understanding the context for their actions is a critical factor in your being able to help them in the best way possible. Second, when someone comes home and is obviously angry, it's a good idea (after they calm down) to stop by their room, note that you heard them sound upset, and ask what happened that made them so angry. Third, issues of race are complicated. Learning more about people of your own race and those different from you can help you better understand the experiences of your residents. For example, in this situation, I learned that African-American students will sometimes enter a period of time where they immerse themselves in their racial culture in response to racism. This is a natural developmental process, not something to be discouraged.

I hope you learn something from my experience. Good luck!

Keep it real,
Garrett

Discussion Questions

1. How many times did Garrett make assumptions in this scenario?
2. What was the result of making these assumptions?
3. How could Garrett have chosen to act differently in each case in which he made an assumption?
4. How likely do you think the incident that happened to Andre would be to occur on your campus?
5. If you were Andre, how do you think you would react?
6. What are multiple reasons why a variety of students sit together in the dining hall?
7. Are any of these more or less valid?
8. What are the most helpful things you learned from this scenario?
9. How will you act differently as an RA, based on this new knowledge?

Resources

Books:

Tatum, B. D. (2003). *Why are all the black kids sitting together in the cafeteria?": And other conversations about race* (2nd. ed.). New York: Basic Books.

Helms, Janet E. (1992). *A race is a nice thing to have: A guide to being a white person, or Understanding the white persons in your life.* Topeka, KS: Content Communications.

Helms, J. (1990) Black and white racial identity: Theory, research and practice. New York: Greenwood.

Torres, V., Howard Hamilton, M., Cooper, D. (2003). *Identity development of diverse populations: Implications for teaching and administration in higher education.* ASHE-ERIC Higher Education Report: 29 (6). San Francisco: Jossey Bass.

Web sites:

ResLife.net—Building positive communities
http://www.reslife.net/html/tools_0603a.html
Diversity Web—AAC&U
http://www.diversityweb.org/index.cfm

Developing A Diversity Mindset: The Ripple Effect
http://www.reslife.net/html/tools_1002a.html
National Coalition Building Institute
http://www.ncbi.org/

Tips on Helping Someone Who Is Upset

1. Ask questions.
2. Listen.
3. Avoid assumptions.
4. Give them time to vent.
5. Don't assume you can solve their problem for them.

9

IGNORING RACIST COMMENTS

Dear Fellow RA,

Hi, my name is Brian. I attend Beagle University (BU)—a racially diverse campus with 25,000 students in the Southeast. We were founded by an eccentric family who owned a beagle rescue and then won a multistate lottery. They decided to endow a small college in their area that was struggling as long as they changed the name to Beagle University. So, here we are today, students at BU. There are beagle statues, beagle portraits, beagle paintings, beagle everything just about everywhere. It's a dog lover's dream come true.

This year has been my first year as an RA and I've really grown a lot from the experience. The biggest way I've grown is in my under-standing of how the use of language can powerfully affect a commu-nity of individuals. At the beginning of the year, I didn't think that racial insults mattered that much as long as the person saying it didn't mean to hurt the other person. Through my experience though, and the honors thesis I wrote for sociology, I came to realize the power of language in a much deeper fashion.

The Situation

At the beginning of the year during the first hall meeting I had with my guys, I noticed some "friendly" insults going around the room—the kind of talk that guys get into to show who is higher in the pecking order; just normal stuff I thought. One guy would call the other "fag." Another guy said to an African-American guy "Aiight boy, get back to the cotton field and start-a-pickin' that cotton." That comment was a little edgy I thought, but I just ignored it and moved on. A few days later, I heard my resident,

Blake, saying the "n" word while passing the door of two African-American residents. Later, I asked Blake why he used that word. He said he was just talking with a friend about a movie he saw. It sounded like a reasonable explanation. Before long though, people on the floor only hung out with people who looked like them; there was very little positive interaction between people of different races or even with guys who had different interests and political views. The rest of the year went OK, but the community on my floor just wasn't what it could have been; in fact, it was a pretty unfriendly environment now that I think about it.

Getting Some Advice

At the end of the year, I met with Dr. Postmodern, my American Studies professor, to talk about the honors thesis I was going to start in the fall. Before we discussed a topic, I talked with him about the comments being made on my floor. He suggested that I spend the summer doing some reflective journaling about my thoughts on what was happening on my floor, and that maybe it could turn into an idea for my thesis. He suggested I think carefully about how the language used in allegedly playful banter among college males might influence and affect the nature of residence hall communities that are multi-racial. I decided it was a good idea.

I started out by thinking about how much of our language focuses on dividing people into categories (majority vs. minority, handicapped vs. able bodied, Black vs. White, fat vs. thin, privileged vs. disadvantaged). Such words deliberately divide, separate, and depersonalize the people behind the category. I then thought about how some words are OK in referring to groups of people, while others are "not politically correct." As I thought about this distinction, I became frustrated with the word "political" being used in this context. The word itself has developed increasingly negative connotations in our society. In addition, to some, "political" suggests an ulterior motive. Politics often focuses on winners and losers. I think it's better to ditch the term "P.C." and instead talk about the use of inclusive language. This conceptualization identifies an important objective—to make people feel that, no matter how they might be categorized by some, there is a place for all in our many communities. I then began to consider how the use of language affects people's thinking and attributions about others different from themselves.

I thought about how in our society, people tend to be rewarded for generalizing based on observation of patterns as a sign of intelligence. Society rewards identifying patterns and relationships. When a child has a bunch of blocks in front of her, she may be asked to put all the blue ones together, or to put all the square ones in a pile. We tend to reinforce putting things into categories. As I pondered this idea further, I wondered about what happens to White children who infer from their parent's comments that African Americans are somehow inferior. How might this affect impressionable White children? Might it lead to them looking for ways to confirm the statement? By pointing to any available evidence, no matter how obscure, White children, who, of course, later become White adults, might form more solidified beliefs that Blacks are inferior—even if they don't openly admit this to themselves or to others or even consciously realize it.

In my journaling, I then took my thoughts to a whole new level. I thought about how a potential barrier to overcoming racism may be that people will resist changing the views they believe are derived from experience, in order to protect their ego and avoid admitting that any generalization they made was either unfounded or incomplete. Admitting that one's beliefs are unfounded may tie into the emotional issue of having to admit intellectual inadequacy. If, instead of emphasizing the ability to support entrenched ideas, we encouraged more balanced consideration of the merits of multiple perspectives, we might eventually start to develop habits in our children that could set the stage for less thinking that could lead to racism in our society. Maybe if we as a society changed our emphasis in how we think about difference, we could then create stronger communities. I know this all may sound deep, but I tried to take an idea and through journaling, extend it out to some logical conclusions.

A Second Try

As the new year began, I had a new group of residents. I remember the first time a guy called another an inappropriate name, I confronted it immediately—I didn't jump down his throat about it, but I suggested that we could be a group of guys who didn't need to put each other down that way. I couldn't go back and change his upbringing, but I could bring to his attention how his language might affect others, depending upon how it was perceived. The next week I did a program with my residents in which I shared a lot of the thoughts I came up with while I was journaling over the summer. It was as if their eyes were opened to a new reality they had not thought of before. Naturally, not everyone saw the validity of every idea I mentioned. Through discussing my ideas as a group, we were able to identify new insights based upon the multiple perspectives shared in the room. We had a really good conversation, and surprisingly enough, the community on my floor that year was very strong. I hope that you will think about all the ways in which language can affect others. Maybe you can even talk about my ideas with your residents.

Lessons Learned

I learned a lot through my RA experience, and by partnering with a faculty member, placed it into a much broader context. Above all, I could see in retrospect that language is a very powerful tool. What might be intended by one as a playful insult, could be perceived by another as wounding. I also learned that residence halls are often the place where residents experience diversity in a deeper way than they ever have, or likely ever will again. We have such an opportunity to educate them through this lived experience! I also learned that when I took the risk to confront someone's language, it led to great conversations among my residents. It also led to a program that was really the intellectual highlight of the year for our discussions as a floor community. I never thought this would be the way that I would grow, but it was, and I'm glad for it. I hope you learn from my experience. Have a great year!

Sincerely yours,
Brian

Discussion Questions

1. Where do you draw the line between letting a comment go and confronting it?
2. What are some effective ways to confront an offensive comment someone else makes?
3. Why might we be tempted to just let offensive comments slide?
4. Why might it be important to confront offensive comments?
5. What kinds of comments are you comfortable confronting? Why?
6. What kinds of comments are you not comfortable confronting? Why?
7. What are some of your reactions to Brian's reflections?
8. What are the most helpful things you learned from this scenario?
9. How will you act differently as an RA, based on this new knowledge?

Resources

ResLife.net—Building positive communities
http://www.reslife.net/html/tools_0603a.html
Diversity Web—AAC&U
http://www.diversityweb.org/index.cfm
Developing A Diversity Mindset: The Ripple Effect
http://www.reslife.net/html/tools_1002a.html
National Coalition Building Institute
http://www.ncbi.org/
Difference is not Deviant
http://www.reslife.net/html/so-now_0703b.html
Human Awareness Programs
http://www.residentassistant.com/programming/humanawareness/Default.htm

Tips on Confronting Hate Speech

1. Whatever you do, don't ignore it.
2. Repeat what the person just said back to them so they can hear how they sounded.

3. Ask the person if they really meant to say that.
4. Ask the speaker if he or she can think of ways their comments might have affected others.
5. Suggest that the individual figure out how to learn from the experience and make necessary amends to others in their community.

10

A CASE OF RELIGIOUS DISCRIMINATION

Dear Fellow RA,

Hi! My name is Joe. I'm an Area Coordinator at West Coast State University. A few years ago, I was in your shoes as an RA at Northern Igloo University. I had such a great experience as an RA that I decided to get my master's degree in higher education, at a great school near the James River in southeast Virginia and pursue a career in student affairs. I highly recommend it! When I was an RA at NIU, my floor lived together through the events of September 11, 2001. As you can imagine, it was quite a year, and quite an experience.

Northern Igloo University is where you might expect it to be, way up north. It gets so cold some days that if you are holding a cup of water in your hand, the water can freeze when you are walking outside from one class to another. Fortunately, we have an underground tunnel system between most academic buildings, so we don't have to face the wind.

The Situation

The guys on my floor got along instantly at the beginning of the year. Of course, they better, because we spend most of our time indoors in close quarters! Everyone had their own personality and experiences growing up, and for some reason we all just fit together really well. As guys do, we developed different nicknames for each other during the first couple weeks of school. Sometimes it would be based on something stupid the guy had done in his past, or a funny thing he managed to pull off in the first week of school. From an outsider's perspective, some of the nicknames might have seemed in poor taste, foul, or disgusting, but to us they made sense and there was no harm done; at least for the most part. Like this one guy we called "colitis," because he spent a lot of time, well, sitting in the bathroom. Another guy we called "gimpy," because he broke his leg during the first week of school trying to impress a senior woman with his dance moves (or lack thereof). Were the nicknames in poor taste? Yes, probably so, to some people, but it was our floor, our community, and that's how we liked it.

September 11, 2001 was a tough day. One of the guys on the floor, Colin, had a cousin who worked in the World Trade Center. Another guy, Josh, had an aunt who worked at the Pentagon. We found out that Josh's aunt made it out alive. We didn't hear that until several hours after the plane crashed, so it was pretty tense for awhile. Hearing about Colin's cousin was a different matter though. It took a week and a half to find out for sure that he died. That was really tough on Colin, and shook up other guys on the floor; most of whom had not dealt with death before.

The events of that day also brought to the surface some underlying tension toward Vishal, a Muslim student who lived on the floor. The guys had nick-named him Osama earlier in the year, after hearing a news report that Osama Bin Laden, who claimed to be Muslim, was planning to bomb the United States. Vishal thought it was funny to be called Osama, especially given the other names for guys on the floor, so it wasn't a big deal. That is, until September 11. Nobody really called him Osama for the first few days after the attacks. About a week later though, as we were still waiting for word on Colin's cousin, one of the guys, Todd, started calling Vishal "terrorist." I thought it was in poor taste, but then again, so were all of the nicknames on the hall, so I let it go. As the week went on, every time Todd and Vishal were in the same room and other people were around, Todd would somehow bring up either September 11 or Islam. He would say things like, "Did you hear that Colin's cousin was killed by a Muslim?" "Hey terrorist, when you pray 5 times a day, are you praying that more people like Colin's cousin will get killed?" "Yo, Osama, do you like being a terrorist?" Vishal started spending less and less time on the floor, and he ended up transferring to a school closer to his hometown.

Getting Some Advice

I went and talked with a minister I knew at the Interfaith Community Center on campus soon after the events of September 11 happened. As I was spending so much time supporting my residents, I needed an outlet where I could go to unload my feelings about all of it. Plus, the events of that day made me rethink my religious beliefs. I was thinking of starting to go to church again, and wasn't sure how I felt about the fact that all the hijackers were Muslim. I ended up talking with Pastor David once a week all semester. It really helped; I grew a lot, and now I have gotten more involved in my church and dedicated my life to Christ. As I talked with Pastor David about how my floor was dealing with everything, it took me a few weeks to talk with him about Vishal, and the whole nickname thing on my floor. It's kind of hard to understand if you don't live on my floor, and even harder to understand if you are a minister I guess. You should have seen his face when I explained to him why we called one of the guys "colitis." Once I got an outsider's perspective on what was happening on my floor, it became clear that our atmosphere—while most considered it jovial—was indeed toxic. Calling someone "Osama" or "terrorist" is hateful. Having an environment where that can be supported is not characteristic of the kind of inclusive community we should have in a residence hall.

A Second Chance

About halfway through the semester, I had a real heart-to-heart with my residents. Unfortunately, Vishal didn't come—he felt so ostracized by the floor by that point that he had socially withdrawn from us, and then withdrew from the school entirely by the end of the semester. I talked with the guys about the difference between the effects of an action and the intentions behind it. We talked about how what can be funny in one context can be damaging in another. We also talked about how our ever more personal and caustic teasing was getting out of hand and ultimately led to a student leaving our community entirely.

Lessons Learned

I learned a lot through that experience about what it means to be an RA, what it means to lead a community, how people experience prejudice based on religious beliefs, and how people sometimes justify prejudice. In retrospect, I can see many of the mistakes I made. I can also see how I was able to engage in extended dialogue with my residents so that they grew as a result. Challenging people's behavior is not easy. It is very difficult. It's also what is expected from a leader. I learned an important lesson about what it means to be a leader throughout all of this. I hope you learn from my experience. Have a great year!

Later,

Joe

Discussion Questions

1. Have you known a group of guys like the ones on Joe's hall?
2. To what extent should RAs participate in, let go, or confront the many different behaviors that were occurring on Joe's floor?
3. What are some decisions that Joe made that you would do differently?
4. What might you do the same?
5. What might Joe have done to keep Vishal from feeling like an outsider?
6. Do you think that this sort of thing could happen on your campus?
7. What are the most helpful things you learned from this scenario?
8. How will you act differently as an RA, based on this new knowledge?

Resources

ResLife.net—Building positive communities
http://www.reslife.net/html/tools_0603a.html

Diversity Web—AAC&U
http://www.diversityweb.org/index.cfm
Developing A Diversity Mindset: The Ripple Effect
http://www.reslife.net/html/tools_1002a.html
National Coalition Building Institute
http://www.ncbi.org/
American College Personnel Association Resources
http://www.myacpa.org/sc/scma/index.html
Campus Resources
http://www.washingtonconsultinggroup.net/

Tips on Dealing with Religious Discrimination

1. Even when residents make comments to or about each other where they "don't mean anything by it," suggest that they think about how it could be interpreted.
2. Think what a person who doesn't live on your floor would assume based on your residents' comments if they heard them out of context.
3. Consider how residents on your floor might really feel on the inside about comments that criticize their religious beliefs; do they really feel safe saying they don't like to be picked on in that way?
4. Consider whether you believe it is appropriate to criticize one's religious beliefs for the purpose of humor.
5. Consider doing a program on your floor about different religions and religious practices to build their respect for each other's spiritual side.

11

THE FACEBOOK NIGHTMARE

Dear Fellow RA,

Hi, my name is JoAnn. I'm a head resident at New England College of Design and Art (NECDA). We live in a cold climate, and spend a lot of time indoors—unless we are going to class or skiing. The skiing here is just incredible; you can go anytime from October to March. We have a lot of students from privileged backgrounds—senators' kids, students whose parents are leaders of business and industry in New York, even a prince from overseas. I have really enjoyed my three years on staff, especially my role as a head resident this year. My first year was a tough one though. Things just got out of hand way too fast on my floor, and we never quite recovered from it. I've turned into an antitechnology person as a result. Let me explain.

The Situation

The women on my floor seemed to get along together well from the beginning, despite some personality conflicts. I had a group of women who were pretty loud and liked to go out to the fraternities, a few athletes who were into staying healthy, and a few residents who were really involved in one of the religious groups on campus. They were quite a mix of residents. At first I thought things would be great. And then they kind of fell apart. Within the first few days, they decided to make a facebook page for the floor. That's cool, I thought, a great way to connect. A few of the louder ladies on the hall agreed to put it together. I could tell when it got brought up at the floor meeting that not everyone was really into it, but most people seemed to be and I figured some were just being a little shy. So, the group got started, and it was named "We live in Reagan First West and you don't, bitches!"

Lots of facebook groups end with the word "bitches" so I didn't even think twice about it. Some of the women on my floor didn't have facebook in high school and were just getting used to the idea. I think a few of them were caught off guard by the name of the group and they didn't register.

At the next floor meeting, the organizers of the facebook group told everyone they had to register by that night, or they'd start making stuff up about them on the facebook page. I thought that was a funny way to get everyone on. Not everyone took it to be funny, but everyone did end up getting on. They developed their own code words for different things; for example "boinking" was hooking up, "studying" meant drinking alcohol. Whenever someone on the floor would hook up, she'd get messages written on her wall asking who she "boinked." They would plan to get together to drink before going out to parties and would send out messages about group "study" sessions on Friday night. Some of the women on the floor actually thought it really meant studying, so they were surprised when they showed up with their books, and everyone else had bottles of tequila. The women who showed up to really study were laughed at pretty hard. The follow up on facebook later was pretty cruel.

Getting Some Advice

The next day I got a call from the Dean of Students. She said she got a call from a state senator demanding to know why his daughter Julia's RA had forced her to join an online "bitch club." Apparently, he was pretty upset about it, as was his daughter. The senator also asked why I was allowing students to have wild tequila parties on the floor. I told the dean about the facebook group (she really didn't understand facebook too well). I know it sounds bad to an outsider, but it is really not that big a deal if you know what facebook is all about. However, I could see her point about how someone else could perceive it. I also let her know that I did hear about a party the night before, and that I was going to address it. The bigger issue was that Julia was really upset by the tension on the floor and how she was being treated. So I went to talk with Julia.

I felt like I really hadn't done my job after hearing how much Julia was upset. She asked why I let the residents on the floor make up a facebook group where everyone was labeled as a "bitch." I told her that was just how some facebook groups are named. The intent is to refer to everyone who is not in the group as bitches. That didn't seem to make her feel much better. Julia also asked why I would let her go to a "study session" with her books that was really a party and have her look like an idiot. I explained to Julia that I had nothing to do with the party on the floor, and could not have prevented what happened. However, I did say that I would work with her and other residents on the floor to mediate the conflict.

A Second Chance

After what seemed like endless one-on-one meetings and group mediations, things finally quieted down on my floor. The facebook group name was changed, and women who didn't really want to be part of it felt more able to not be on it if they chose. We talked about how each person had her own comfort level with different social activities, and different labels, and how we all needed to be considerate of that. The rest of the year wasn't exactly great, but it was a lot less tense.

Lessons Learned

As with many things as an RA, I learned that you need to trust that gut feeling in your stomach when something seems not quite right. When that happens to you, just ask a question. You don't even need to say "This sounds wrong, don't do it." You could just say "I wonder if everyone is comfortable with this idea." Sometimes clearing the air, or setting up an environment where everyone feels comfortable requires that you act on your instincts. When the facebook group started, I should have been more proactive to see that everyone was comfortable with it. I could tell when it was brought up that they weren't; I wish now that I had said something before things spiraled out of control. I hope you learn from my experience. Have a great year!

In solidarity,
JoAnn

Discussion Questions

1. What were several decision points that JoAnn had when the facebook situation was starting off?
2. Where could she have said something that could have prevented hurt feelings later?
3. How much should an RA be responsible for the groups that residents create on facebook?
4. When should the RA say something about a facebook group involving residents?
5. Is it spying when an RA looks at a resident's facebook group?
6. What should an RA do when there are facebook pictures of residents breaking policy?
7. What are the most helpful things you learned from this scenario?
8. How will you act differently as an RA, based on this new knowledge?

Resources

Your Online Life—ResLife.net
http://www.reslife.net/html/so-now_0805a.html
Higher Education Information Technology Alliance
http://www.heitalliance.org/
The Campus Computing Project
http://www.campuscomputing.net/
Campus Technology Magazine
http://www.campus-technology.com/index.asp
Online Social Networking: Training Our Staff as Role Models
http://www.reslife.net/html/technology_0206a.html
Student Affairs OnLine—The online magazine about technology and Student Affairs
http://studentaffairs.com/ejournal

Tips for Online Safety

1. Talk openly with your residents about what they put online about themselves.

2. Encourage your residents to be discreet about putting personal information online.

3. Encourage residents to use the safety tools provided on Web sites to decrease the chances of someone they don't want seeing their personal information doing so.

4. Don't hesitate to call out your residents when you think something is happening that might snowball into a big mess.

5. Model the behavior you think your residents should practice.

PART 3

RESIDENT SUPPORT

CHAPTER 12 ASSUMING THAT A FIRST-YEAR STUDENT WHO OUTWARDLY SEEMS TO HAVE IT ALL TOGETHER DOESN'T NEED ANY HELP OR SUPPORT

CHAPTER 13 NOT CONFRONTING A STUDENT WHO SERVES OTHERS SO MUCH THAT SHE HURTS HERSELF

CHAPTER 14 NOT REACHING OUT TO A LONELY RESIDENT

CHAPTER 15 TELLING A RESIDENT'S PARENT THAT IT IS OK TO CALL YOU

CHAPTER 16 COMMUNICATING WITH A RESIDENT OVER INSTANT MESSENGER INSTEAD OF HAVING A CONVERSATION

CHAPTER 17 KEEPING YOUR RELATIONSHIPS WITH RESIDENTS IN BALANCE

Supporting your residents as they try to fit in, to help others relate to their parents, make decisions about policy, and decide how to relate to you can be very challenging for RAs. Bob's experience in chapter 12 shows us that not every resident knows how to ask for support, but they all need it one way or another. Shannon and her dealings with a resident who worked so hard for others that she burned out herself teaches us much about how to reach such residents in chapter 13.

Next, we learn from Chuck about the importance of reaching out to lonely residents in chapter 14. Chapter 15 teaches a valuable lesson about when not to say "yes" to a request for help—something that Jake learned the hard way. Next, in chapter 16, Kara tries to confront a policy violation by IM'ing a resident she didn't want to confront in person. Surely there is much we can all learn from that situation. Finally, Peter gives us all great advice on how to establish boundaries between our residents and ourselves.

12

ASSUMING THAT A FIRST-YEAR STUDENT WHO OUTWARDLY SEEMS TO HAVE IT ALL TOGETHER DOESN'T NEED ANY HELP OR SUPPORT

Dear Fellow RA,

Hi. My name is Bob. Last year was my first year as an RA. I attend Large State University (LSU)—a school of about 40,000 students in the Midwest. LSU is a school in a big college town with lots to do. You can major in just about anything at LSU and there are 400 student organizations to choose from—never a lack of options. Lots of people really like it here. Occasionally, someone slips through the cracks though. That's what happened to one of my residents last year, Dan. It caught me totally off guard. I hope that by hearing this story, you'll be better prepared so it doesn't happen with one of your residents.

The Situation

A couple days before first-year student move in day, Dan moved in to start practicing with the track team. He was the only athlete on my floor. I ran into him after RA training one day, and was surprised to have a resident there. Once I realized that he was cleared to have moved in, I let him know that I was his RA and would be happy to help him out if he ever needed anything. He was quick to tell me that he went to boarding school, so he knew what college would be like, and that he'd be just fine. I took him at his word. That was a mistake.

I should have known better. Actually, I did know better, I just didn't think it through.

Dan was away for most of Orientation week when everyone was getting to know each other. I just figured he had track practice. Some of the time that was true; I later found out that a lot of the rest of the time he was just off by himself running or spending time with his high school girlfriend. I saw Dan maybe once a week or so—which was odd because most of my residents I saw every day. Guys on the floor referred to him as the "ghost resident" because they hardly saw him. I had a wrestler on my floor last year, and he hung out a lot with his teammates and seemed to be fine, so I figured Dan was just doing about the same.

It turns out that with Dan being away so much during Orientation, he felt left out when he would come back after track practice. He was shy by nature and tended to keep people at a distance, so most guys didn't get to know him much. I later realized that what he needed was to know that I was really there for him; he also needed someone who would make the extra effort to be sure he met people when he was around.

Dan thought that boarding school taught him everything he needed to know about college life. That turned out to be wrong. He struggled socially his first year, and did not do well in class—particularly in calculus. He almost failed it; he squeaked by with a D. He came back the second semester on academic probation and was really down, and more than just a little bit embarrassed about the whole thing.

Getting Some Advice

My Resident Director (RD), met with each of us at the beginning of the semester to talk about how the fall had been and what our plans were with our residents for the spring semester. I told him more about Dan, and we talked about ways to support him. I realized that I shouldn't have let Dan off the hook at the beginning of the year with a "leave me alone, I'll be OK" comment that he gave me. I knew better. I decided to make Dan a focus of my efforts during the spring semester.

A Second Chance

Getting his first D ever really woke Dan up. He had no idea what to do. I waited around for him after track practice one day, and asked him to grab dinner with me. He was hesitant at first, but agreed to do so. About half way through dinner, he just started unloading. He talked about being so nervous about college, about how he kept people at a distance so they couldn't tell he needed help, and how he was really scared about how he would do in his classes that spring. He talked about feeling awkward on the floor, and how he wished he knew more people but thought it was too late. I encouraged him to hang out more on the hall, and said I'd plan some times where he'd have a logical excuse to hang out. I suggested he start an intramural floor hockey team with the guys. They were surprised to hear him ask, but they liked the idea. They really got to know him better, and he felt a lot better about the floor and himself. I also got him in to see someone at the writing center to help out with his paper writing. By the end of the semester, he had earned much better grades.

Lessons Learned

I learned a lot about what it takes to reach out to different kinds of residents. In particular, I learned that there are some guys who put on airs that everything is OK because they don't want to admit that they need any help. So many guys are raised to be tough, independent, and not take help from anyone that they end up flailing around aimlessly. I really wish I had seen through the gruff exterior with which Dan started the year. I won't make that same mistake again. In a few days, my new residents move in for another year. This time, I'm much more ready. I hope you learn from my experience. Have a great year!

Adios,
Bob

Discussion Questions

1. Why might Dan have been standoffish at the beginning of the year?
2. Are students who have been to boarding school better off in getting used to college than other residents?
3. What could Bob have done to make Dan feel more included during the beginning of the year?
4. What could Bob have done to better support Dan early in the year?
5. If you were sitting down with Bob during his first week as an RA and you wanted to be sure that he supported Dan well, what would you say to him?
6. How would you deal with a resident like Dan?
7. What are the most helpful things you learned from this scenario?
8. How will you act differently as an RA, based on this new knowledge?

Resources

Living and Working with Freshmen Residents
http://www.reslife.net/html/tools_0903a.html
National Resource Center for the First-Year Experience and Students in Transition
http://www.sc.edu/fye/

Tips on Helping Residents

1. Not everyone will ask for help; some need to be asked.
2. With some first-year students, you have to peel back their rough exterior to get to their point of need.
3. Make sure your residents who "always have it together" always know you are there for them.
4. Model vulnerability. Be sure residents know that you don't always have it all together.
5. Help residents know how to find answers for themselves.

13

Not Confronting a Student Who Serves Others so Much that She Hurts Herself

Dear Fellow RA,

Hi! My name is Shannon. I'm an RA at Highland Community College. I know, you didn't think that community colleges had residence halls. We were actually the first community college to start up a residence life program. Now more and more community colleges are putting residence halls on their campuses. We led the way in that, and are very proud of doing so. I just finished my year as an RA at HCC, and am transferring to a great school, Beagle University, for next year. Before I pack my things up though, I am writing you this letter to talk about the biggest mistake I made in the past year. I hope that by reading it, you'll not repeat the same mistake that I made.

The Situation

Shelley was my most energetic resident this year. She was the kind of person who was always, and I mean always, there for everyone. She just poured herself into everything here at HCC doing outreach programs for the community, running study sessions on our floor, starting new student organizations on campus, that sort of thing. She was always on the go! I never really worried about her at all because she seemed to have it all together, and was such a burst of energy for my floor!

During midterms, I sensed something was not quite right with Shelley. I had this feeling in my gut, which in retrospect I should have paid attention to at the time. Unlike everyone else who was studying hard, Shelley would study for a few minutes, and then someone would come in her room asking for help and she'd tutor them for hours. She'd then go host a study break for one of her student organizations, and then put in a few volunteer hours at the local women's shelter. I asked Shelley how she was doing one day and she said, "Going in a million directions but helping lots of people, so it is worth it!" I really admired her drive to serve others.

It turns out that in serving others so much, she ended up not taking good enough care of herself. She wound up getting mostly Cs and Ds on her midterms. Her grades were not a good reflection of her ability—she just worked so hard to help others that she didn't study for her own tests. Right around when she got her grades back, she caught a bad case of mono, and ended up just barely making it through the rest of the semester. Her first semester grades were horrible.

Over the holiday break, I thought a lot about Shelley. She actually reminded me of myself when I was her age. One day as I was visiting relatives and started letting my mind wander to thoughts about school, I realized that Shelley had not yet learned that important lesson I learned last year. In order to serve others, you first must take good care of yourself. It was a tough lesson for me to learn, as I am also someone who is inclined to help others in any way I can. However, I discovered that people like me and Shelley can work so hard to help others that we neglect ourselves. In this case, Shelley's care for others jeopardized her status as a student and really hurt her health.

A Second Chance

When the new semester started, I sat down with Shelley and had a long conversation about her semester, and how great it was that she served others so much, but how much it was hurting her. She was pretty defensive at first, but in the end, couldn't argue much with the facts before her—her grades and poor health. We spent time together figuring out what she could still do to serve others, and what new things she needed to do to make sure she earned better grades and stayed healthier. It wasn't an easy transition for her, but it was one she needed to go through. I'm just glad that I understood how she felt, as I had to do the same thing.

Lessons Learned

It is easy to remember to do lots of the things we do as RAs. Fill out those Room Condition Reports, document violations of policy, do your programs, check in with the residence life office, make sure you show up on time for duty, etc. But there is more than the obvious stuff to being an RA. Some of it is rather subtle, and you have to learn to pick up on the nuances. In this case, I learned that even the residents who you think might need you the least, really need you the most. Everyone needs an RA, especially during their first year of college. Sometimes what they need most is direction toward more ethical behavior, sometimes they need help establishing good study habits, and sometimes they need a reminder to take care of themselves. It is our job to figure out what residents need, and do our best to help them get their needs met. And of course, along the way, we need to remember to take care of ourselves too. As you go through your first year as an RA, I hope you will recognize residents like Shelley and will be faster to give them this kind of advice than I was. I hope you learn from my experience. Have a great year!

With a caring heart,
Shannon

Discussion Questions

1. How can we know when students like Shelley need our help?
2. Why can it be tempting to assume that they don't need our advice?
3. What are some possible ways that we can approach students like Shelley to help them see the importance of taking care of themselves?
4. Have you known any students like Shelley before?

5. If so, are they still acting like Shelley did, or did they find balance after awhile?
6. What do you do to maintain balance?
7. How can you avoid going to the extreme that Shelley went to?
8. What are the most helpful things you learned from this scenario?
9. How will you act differently as an RA, based on this new knowledge?

Resources

Carol Gilligan
http://www.webster.edu/~woolflm/gilligan.html

Tips on Helping the Helping Resident

1. Ask your residents what they've done for themselves lately.
2. Ask your residents how much sleep they are getting.
3. If you notice a resident whose personal responsibilities are slipping because they are serving others so much, let them know that you can tell something isn't right.
4. Reward residents for helping others, but remind them that in order to best help others, they must take care of themselves.
5. Model good behavior by taking care of yourself, too!

14

NOT REACHING OUT TO
A LONELY RESIDENT

Dear Fellow RA,

Hi. My name is Chuck. During my sophomore and junior year, I was an RA for first-year men. This year I live off campus with a few friends. I go to a small liberal arts college in Pennsylvania, Ryon University. Here at R.U. we have a small, close-knit community of students. Almost everyone lives on campus. Most of our students did all right in high school, nothing too stellar. Business and English are the most popular majors. One of my apartment-mates this year is Will. He was actually one of my residents two years ago. Back then, I could never imagine living with him. Last night, Will told me how much I hurt him his freshman year. I was shocked.

The Situation

Sophomore year, my hall was "that hall." My guys were the ones who were written up the first night of school for having a keg party. A few days later they were the first hall on campus to have a hall t-shirt. Of course it proclaimed with pride "Carnegie First Lower: Busted First Night!" The next weekend a few of them threw the lounge furniture out a third story window. One guy broke a sink in the bathroom, which broke the building's stack-pipe and ended up flooding several rooms on every floor (seriously, if you looked at the stairs, 3 inches of water on each stair tumbled down three stories; it was quite a sight, and actually looked pretty cool even though it was really destructive). Another weekend, someone lit balls of newspaper on fire and threw them out a few different windows, setting a bush on fire and almost setting the roof on fire (we never did find out who that was). I had one resident who was dealing drugs, another who got into fights with "townies" at least once a month, and another who threatened to kill himself every few weeks. So needless to say, I spent a lot of time with my Area Coordinator figuring things out and with the Dean, too. They kept saying how great a job I was doing despite the circumstances, and that one day I'd be glad that I had so much experience. That day has yet to come.

Somehow Will, my current roommate and resident from that first year I was an RA, got lost in the shuffle of all of this. I was so consumed with the residents I had who were acting out that I lost track of Will. Will was the guy who came in on move-in day and didn't talk to anyone. He just set up his room and went about his business. He went to all the sessions during Orientation, seemed to register for classes OK, and didn't bother anyone. When you saw him in the hallway, he nodded to acknowledge your presence, but he rarely spoke. He spent a lot of time in his room. The only thing I ever heard about him really was from his former roommate, who called him "Weird Willy."

Getting Some Advice

I never expected the best advice I had about my RA experience to come two years later from one of my residents. It turns out Will was really lonely his freshman year. I, who should have noticed, didn't give it a second thought. Will's parents and he didn't get along very well, so Will paid his way through school by working and taking out loans. He came to move-in day alone and had hoped to meet people. Unfortunately, he was so shy that he didn't really talk with anyone, so nobody really talked with him. Now three years later, he told me that one time he heard me ask his roommate how "Weird Willy" was. Will said when he heard that, it made him feel like everyone must have thought he was weird, if even his RA referred to him that way. When he told me I felt like I'd been hit in the head with a baseball, right between the eyes. I felt so bad that I had hurt him that way, especially when he needed some friends. He obviously got over it, as we are living together this year. Will ended up joining some student organizations during his sophomore year and started doing research with a professor who took him under his wing. All in all, the mistake I made could have been a lot worse. Considering the hall I had, I figure it is a miracle that no one died that year. However, with all the activity that was happening, I forgot that a big part of what we as RAs do is reach out to those who need to be encouraged to be part of the social network of the floor. It is the RA who needs to check in with everyone to see how they are doing, even those who are a little different or who don't draw a lot of attention to themselves.

A Second Chance

This year I have the chance to make it up to Will. He's more involved now, but still needs that extra push to get him to connect with people. I'd like to think that I do that for him now, even though I'm no longer on staff. And sometimes, he likes to be alone, and that is OK. But other times, he just needs to be asked to be included and he really appreciates it. It's not that hard.

Lessons Learned

As hard as you try to be the "perfect RA" it just isn't going to happen. You'll find when you look back on the year that you made some mistakes along the way. Knowing that the mistakes will come is no reason to let them happen if they can be avoided. In my case, I really wish I had looked out for Will from the beginning of the year. I especially wish I hadn't called him "Weird Willy"—a move I now recognize was hurtful. Remember that it is your responsibility to look out for all of your residents. I hope you learn from my experience. Have a great year on staff!

In strength,
Brad

Discussion Questions

1. What are some things a resident might do, or not do, that can tell you that they are lonely?
2. What are some strategies for reaching out to all different kinds of students on your floor?
3. What are some ways you can respond when you hear residents developing derogatory nicknames about each other?
4. What are some of the things Brad could have done to notice what was going on with Will sooner?
5. What are some of the reasons why it is important to reach out to students like Will?
6. What might some of the consequences be of not reaching out to students like Will?
7. What are the most helpful things you learned from this scenario?
8. How will you act differently as an RA, based on this new knowledge?

Resources

Campus Blues—Homesickness
http://www.campusblues.com/homesickness.asp
Go Ask Alice!
http://www.goaskalice.columbia.edu/1785.html
ResLife.net—Homesickness Programs
http://www.reslife.net/html/pwithp_0900a.html
Living and Working with Freshmen Residents
http://www.reslife.net/html/tools_0903a.html
National Resource Center for the First-Year Experience and Students in Transition
http://www.sc.edu/fye/

Tips on Helping Shy Residents

1. Some residents cry out for help; some have to be asked. Remember, especially with first-year and transfer students, they all need you!

2. Many residents will make fun of people who are different. Be a good role model.

3. Don't give up on a resident just because he or she says to leave them alone at first.

4. Organize a program during the middle of the first semester for residents to share their frustrations with midterms, etc.

5. Remember to help them relieve stress in healthy ways! Organize a hike or other physical activity.

15

TELLING A RESIDENT'S PARENT THAT IT IS OK TO CALL YOU

Dear Fellow RA,

Howdy. My name is Jake. I'm a senior at Lake George College, a midsized college in the South. Lake George College is located, as you might have guessed, right near Lake George—a beautiful 100 acre lake in the mountains of Appalachia. It is just gorgeous here. Our school has been around for about 100 years, and is mostly a liberal arts college for students who were in the "Second Tier" (25–50th percentile) of their high school graduating class.

I grew up about 50 miles from campus here in the South, where we believe in hospitality, respect for our elders, and being ladies and gentlemen. I've been an RA ever since my sophomore year, and for the most part I've had a great experience doing it. I hit a few bumps in the road my first year on staff though.

The Situation

I was pumped for opening day just like everyone. My school really works hard to make our new students and their families feel at home here. "Always leave them with a smile" is our motto for opening weekend and throughout the year too come to think of it. One of my residents, Brandon Dylanski, went to the same private high school as I did. We didn't know each other too well, but our families were friends and I felt a special responsibility to make him feel at home here. So, I went out of my way to help him unload his stuff, make his parents feel like he was in good hands, that kind of thing. His dad asked me lots of questions that day—where he should go to buy an extension cord, when family weekend was, if we had any extra storage on the hall—the typical parent stuff. I did everything I could to help, and he felt much obliged. Toward the end of the day, Brandon's dad came down to my room and asked if he could have my phone number so he could call from time to time to just see how Brandon was doing. I remembered my Resident Director telling us not to give out our phone numbers to parents, but this was someone who knew my family so I figured it wouldn't be a problem. I gave him my number. He handed me $100, which I gave back to him saying he didn't need to pay me for anything; it was my job to be a good RA.

The calls started the next day. Mr. Dylanski called just to be sure that Brandon was going to all of his Orientation sessions. I assured him he was and he had nothing to worry about. Then he called on the first day of classes to see if Brandon got up early enough for his first class. Then he called on Sunday night as the first weekend was ending to make sure Brandon hadn't partied too much. I started letting his calls just go to voicemail and calling him back with an innocuous answer when I figured he wouldn't be home to answer the phone. I thought he'd get the hint after awhile. He didn't.

Mr. Dylanski called me from a different phone line so I didn't recognize the number, and I answered it. He laid into me like nobody's business. He let me know that I was to respond to all of his calls within an hour of receiving them, that I was to update him with full details about everything he asked about, and that if I didn't he'd see to it that the president of the college heard about my "insubordination." I didn't quite know what to say, so I apologized and got off the phone as soon as I could.

Getting Some Advice

At that point, I went and talked with my Resident Director. I should have talked to him a long time before that point, as I now know. I explained everything that happened. We talked about why it was important that I should have done what I was trained to do, and why I didn't. I got the message, mostly through my bad experience really.

We decided that the next time Mr. Dylanski called, I would forward the call to my Resident Director.

A Second Chance

Sure enough, Mr. Dylanski called about an hour later to ask a question. I told him that I'd need to transfer his call to my supervisor, which I did. They talked things out and Mr. Dylanski didn't call me again. I feel bad about the whole situation, because if I had just explained things to Mr. Dylanski from the start, this whole thing wouldn't have gotten out of hand.

Lessons Learned

Sometimes as an RA it can feel like we are supposed to be all things to all people. We are not. That would be impossible. Our first responsibility is to our residents. Forming an alliance with their parents undermines our relationship the resident, and helps nobody. In my desire to be helpful, I ended up setting an expectation with Mr. Dylanski that wasn't helpful to him or to Brandon—it certainly wasn't helpful to me! Brandon needed to learn how to adapt to college on his own, without his father making sure I was reminding him of every paper deadline, getting him out of bed, etc. I hope you learn from my experience. Have a great year on staff!

All my best,
Jake

Discussion Questions

1. What are some reasons why it is important not to give parents your phone number?
2. What are some reasons why it is important to follow the procedures you are told to follow by your supervisor?
3. What could Jake have said to Mr. Dylanski to explain why he couldn't give out his phone number?

4. What could Jake have done if Mr. Dylanski didn't understand why he couldn't have Jake's phone number?
5. How might Mr. Dylanski's having Jake's phone number affected Jake's relationship with Brandon?
6. What are the most helpful things you learned from this scenario?
7. How will you act differently as an RA, based on this new knowledge?

Tips on Parents

1. Your primary relationship is with your resident, not parents; keep it that way.
2. If a parent asks you for information you shouldn't give them, be polite and tell them how they can get what they need (from their son or daughter or a professional staff member).
3. Never give a parent your phone number.
4. If a parent is insistent, give them your supervisor's contact information.
5. Tell your resident if you receive communication from their parent; keep the resident informed and be sure they know you are on "their side."

16

COMMUNICATING WITH A RESIDENT OVER INSTANT MESSENGER INSTEAD OF HAVING A CONVERSATION IN PERSON

Dear Fellow RA,

Hi! My name is Kara. This is my second year as an RA at Western State University. We are a large public institution in an urban area on the west coast. I just love it here at WSU. We have so much to do, so many things to see near our campus, an exciting night life. We also have lots to get involved with on campus. Most people here major in accounting, psychology, or biology. A few people major in English, and the rest is divided up in the other liberal arts. WSU was my first choice of schools to attend; I can't imagine going anywhere else!

From my first week of school I decided I wanted to be an RA. I just knew that having a hall would be just awesome. I wasn't sure if I wanted first-year students or upper-class students. I applied and got hired and was assigned a floor of upper-class women. It was a tough transition as some of my residents were two years older than me. That was intimidating, but I made it through the year OK. Except for this one incident...

The Situation

Tonya was a very assertive woman who lived on my floor. She was a senior and was a starter on the women's basketball team. Lots of people knew her, she was well liked, and she had an active social life.

She was a great person to be around, except when she was in one of those moods where she didn't feel like talking to you. If she didn't want to talk with you, she would just lash out and tell you to get out of her face.

One day my Resident Director called me to say that one of my residents had a piece of furniture in her room that was against university regulations. He told me that I needed to tell the resident to get rid of the item. I was just hoping it was anyone but Tonya, but of course, it was she. My RD said I needed to talk with Tonya about it and explain why it was a problem. To be honest, I really can't stand confrontation. I avoid it whenever possible. So, when my RD told me I had to talk with Tonya, I really didn't want to do it face to face. I decided to IM her when I knew she was in her room, so that we could talk about it that way so in case she was mad I wouldn't have to deal with it.

So I noticed that Tonya was in her room after a basketball practice and a few minutes later I IM'ed her and said "Hey Tonya." She didn't respond right away so I wrote "You need to get the couch out of your room in the next 24 hours or you could get evicted." A couple minutes later I could hear Tonya yelling in her room. It was a combination of obscenities and my name, so I was really glad that I had IM'ed her instead of talking with her, for a moment anyway. She then sent me a message that I'd rather not put in writing, but suffice it to say, she was annoyed with me and made it clear that the only way her couch was leaving her room was if I was standing outside her room and she threw it on my head. The whole situation deteriorated from there, and I just gave up. I figured Tonya would calm down and get rid of the couch on her own and that the problem would just go away by itself. Who cares about an illegal couch in a resident's room anyway? What's the big deal? I figured I had a lot more important things to attend to, and I surely didn't want to have a confrontation with Tonya.

Getting Some Advice

The next month, my RD said there had been another inspection on my floor, and Tonya still had an illegal couch in her room. He asked me if Tonya had removed it the first time I asked her. At that point I had to 'fess up and tell him what I had done. I realized after talking with my RD that I had put both myself and Tonya in a bad position. First, at a minimum, I should have talked with Tonya after our IM exchange. Second, I looked foolish to my RD because I hadn't done an effective job the first time.

A Second Chance

I ended up going to talk with Tonya in person. She was still annoyed with me, but after breaking through her gruff exterior, we had a good conversation about it. It can be hard to confront someone in person about something, but it is even harder when you do so using technology that does not allow the other person to hear the tone of your voice, see that you care about them but need them to do something, nor connect with that individual on a personal level.

Lessons Learned

I learned from Tonya that she can't stand it when people write her notes or IM her about things she thinks they should say to her face. I let her know that I was intimidated by her when she got angry. She explained that it was just her way of communicating, but that she appreciated knowing how she was affecting me. We had a really good, thorough conversation about it. Sometimes it can seem more efficient to IM someone about something you need them to do. In the end, it is far more effective to have a talk about it in person, face to face. It is a lesson I learned the hard way. I hope you will learn from my experience. Have a great year!

Warm good wishes,
Kara

Discussion Questions

1. Is it ever OK for an RA to IM their residents? When?
2. When is it not a good idea to IM a resident?

3. What benefits do face-to-face communication have over electronic communication?

4. What would you do if a resident IM'ed you something that you thought you should talk about in person?

5. Is it ever advisable to continue that conversation online?

6. How do you know when it is best to have an in-person conversation versus one that is online?

7. What are the most helpful things you learned from this scenario?

8. How will you act differently as an RA, based on this new knowledge?

Resources

Your Online Life—ResLife.net
http://www.reslife.net/html/so-now_0805a.html
Higher Education Information Technology Alliance
http://www.heitalliance.org/
The Campus Computing Project
http://www.campuscomputing.net/
Campus Technology Magazine
http://www.campus-technology.com/index.asp

Tips for Online Safety

1. Remind your residents about the dangers of giving personal information out online.

2. Caution residents about agreeing to meet people who approach them online.

3. Suggest that if your residents have a conflict with someone that they discuss it in person, not online.

4. Use online resources carefully when communicating with residents.

5. Model "in person" communication with residents whenever possible.

17

Keeping Your Relationships with Residents in Balance

Dear Fellow RA,

Hi. My name is Peter. I'm a junior at a highly competitive public school of around 6,000 students, Eastern State University. Most students at ESU live on campus in the residence halls; we are known for having a really strong campus community. My advice to you in this letter is not so much the result of a particular difficult situation, it's more a compilation of my reflections on keeping your relationships with your residents in balance. Sometimes it is tempting to do too much for them, or to get closer to them than would be best for your RA role. This is a bit of my experience for you to take or leave as you will.

The Situation

If I had to comment on what the most challenging aspect of being an RA was, I would probably choose to discuss the huge balancing act that new RAs bring on themselves when they assume the responsibilities of a student staff position. Especially with first-year halls, it is all too easy to absorb yourself into a role that really has no definite upper limit. When you mix that with the standard responsibilities of any college student (other activities, leadership positions, friends, and classes), it can set you up for burning out. One of the biggest mistakes I made as a first year RA was letting the job consume all of me at points. I mean it just took over everything. While there is no specific "situation" I have to tell you about, here are many different parts of being an RA that took on more control of my life than needed to be the case.

Getting Some Advice

Unlike many other letters in this book, I'll simply give some advice to you from experience, rather then tell you about advice I got from others. Being an RA is a rewarding position to hold, despite the challenges it brings. Like anything in life, it's important to keep it in perspective and balance. In essence, sometimes you can become like the giving tree of the well-known children's book when you choose being there for your residents or getting to know them better rather than dealing with your other obligations. It's a little too easy sometimes to shrug off a paper and just walk around the hall to get caught up with everyone, put up a bulletin board, or work on all the lovely paperwork that inevitably finds its way to you at all times of the year. Another side effect of this common error is developing the expectation of residents that you will always be there. I can remember thinking during the spring semester as I began to push residents to do things for themselves and use the campus resources to accomplish what they needed to get done that they should be developing more autonomy as they were getting ready to finish their first year. It dawned on me as I arranged a taxi for a resident toward the end of spring break that maybe I was willing to step in and help too much and was not encouraging my residents to do things for themselves enough. I think a lot of us who are drawn to the position are quick to step in and do things for others, rather than help them figure out how to do them for themselves.

In the same vein of keeping everything in balance, the relationships you build with residents can also be prone to some tensions if you're not careful. As an RA for first-year men, I found it pretty typical to be around quite a bit during the fall semester. The demands of the job and your outside obligations often make the community on your hall one of the most immediate circles of people with whom you associate regularly. It's great to develop friendships with your residents, but it's also important to remain cognizant of your role as an RA versus your role as a friend to your residents (especially should there be a time in the future when the two would conflict). It's important to keep the two separate at some level; this in itself can be a strain on those friendships, even without having any confrontations regarding policy. Toward the end of the year, I had a lot of tension with a group of my residents with whom I became very good friends about their frustration with my not committing to them more strongly as their friend. I feel like I couldn't fully offer myself in a friendship because of the restraints of what the job asked of me. Not respecting this sort of barrier can have a negative effect on your ability to serve as an authority figure with your residents. I found that experiencing this barrier was very frustrating, but can also be a test of how meaningful a friendship is.

A Second Chance

Now that I'm in my second year as an RA, I'm doing things differently. I'm very friendly with my residents, but am more careful about giving away my friendship so freely. I also am less likely to do things for my residents, and am more likely to help them meet their own goals. Sometimes it may seem easier to do it for them, but in the end, they will grow the best if you guide them in doing things for themselves.

Lessons Learned

I'm so glad I served as an RA. It taught me a lot about responsibility and how best to help others. It taught me that doing things for people doesn't help them nearly as much as supporting them through making their own decisions. It taught me that when you are in a leadership role, there are going to be awkward moments and other difficulties in being friends with those whom you lead. That is all part of growing up. Being an RA is hard. It is also one of the most rewarding things you can do in college. I'd recommend it to almost anyone who has the skills to do the job, and who wants to embark on an adventure they will look back on as a time when they grew and changed the most during college. Of course, some of that change can be painful, but isn't most growth painful in some way? I think so. I hope you got something out of my advice and experience. Have a great year.

Yours always,
Peter

Discussion Questions

1. Where is the line drawn between "friend" and "resident"?
2. Why should there be a line?
3. Is this line different for different RAs?
4. Is this line different for different residents?
5. What might happen if that line is different for some residents than others?
6. What might be the consequences of having your primary friendship group be your residents?
7. Is that a good idea? Why or why not?
8. What other things are important to keep in balance as an RA?
9. What are the most helpful things you learned from this scenario?
10. How will you act differently as an RA, based on this new knowledge?

Resources

You hold the key: The RA/Friend Relationship
http://www.reslife.net/html/so-now_1002a.html
The Ultimate Ethical Dilemma of an RA: Friendship or Policy?
http://www.reslife.net/html/so-now_0203a.html
Creating Boundaries
http://www.reslife.net/html/tools_0803b.html
Take Care of YOU!
http://www.residentassistant.com/advice/careofyou.htm

Tips on Staying Balanced

1. Most of the time, it is best to show residents how to solve their own problems, rather than doing it for them.
2. Schedule time away from your residents to stay refreshed.
3. Be very careful about being "friends" with your residents. Be friendly, be helpful, but remember your role as leader of your area.
4. When conflict arises between you and residents, talk it out.

5. Be sure your supervisor knows how things are going with your residents; it is amazing the great advice they can give you about how best to cope!

PART 4
POLICY ENFORCEMENT

CHAPTER 18 "IF I CAN'T SEE IT, IT ISN'T THERE": A DANGEROUS WAY TO AVOID POLICY ENFORCEMENT

CHAPTER 19 ENJOYING POLICY ENFORCEMENT TOO MUCH

CHAPTER 20 ENFORCING POLICY SELECTIVELY: HOW TO REALLY ANNOY YOUR RESIDENTS

CHAPTER 21 IGNORING ESCALATING DOMESTIC VIOLENCE

CHAPTER 22 ASSUMING A RESIDENT WHO COMES HOME DRUNK FREQUENTLY CAN HANDLE THEIR ALCOHOL

CHAPTER 23 ASSUMING THAT ALL STUDENTS WHO APPEAR INTOXICATED WERE DRINKING ALCOHOL AND NOT USING OTHER DRUGS

Policy enforcement is a tough part of the RA role. Few actually enjoy doing it (nobody should *enjoy* it per se). Some avoid it. Some do it well. All of us need to find our own style and do it effectively. Of course, it is critical that you decide how you will confront a violation before you get into your first rough situation, so that you have an idea about how to proceed. It is difficult, but necessary. As we learn in chapter 18 from Scott, shirking responsibility is a poor choice. On the other end of the continuum, Christopher shows us in chapter 19 that getting too heavily into "busting" people for the fun of it is not an effective attitude for our role as educators. In the dangerous middle of that continuum is the approach chosen by Linda in chapter 20. Through her experience we learn that inconsistency can land you in a heap of trouble! In chapter 21, we get into a specific type of policy enforcement that, if done well, can help protect a resident from serious harm. Chapter 22 details the poor choices of Jason, who ended up losing his staff position given his inability to properly enforce policy. An incident in chapter 23 with Claire's residents shows us that we need to question our assumptions about what kind of drug (alcohol or other drugs) our residents are using. Given the serious harm, even death, that can result from abuse of drugs and not following policy, it is critical that we all understand this role and perform it to the utmost of our ability.

18

"If I Can't See It, It Isn't There"

A Dangerous Way to Avoid Policy Enforcement

Dear Fellow RA,

My name is Scott. I just graduated from Social State University. As you might have already guessed, SSU is a place where you can always find a party. A national magazine has rated us in the top three party schools in the nation for the last five years in a row. That is not exactly something our residence life staff is proud of, but it is a reality that we deal with day in and day out.

I had always wanted to be an RA ever since I visited my older brother when he was in college and I was in 10th grade. I thought his RA was so cool—he hung out with them, let the little stuff slide, and lived by the motto "If I can't see it, it isn't there." College was going to be great; and I would make it great for a lot of people, or so I thought. I got to college and my RA was kind of, well, a dork. There is really no other way to say it. He never let us get away with anything. So, inspired by my boring first year of college, I applied to be an RA and I got the job.

The Situation

I couldn't wait for my guys to move in. They started arriving around 7 a.m. on opening day. I kind of felt sorry for the ones whose parents were there at the front door by 6 a.m. I could tell they were ready to ditch the 'rents quickly. By the end of the morning, all my residents were there, all coming to me with questions, trying to figure out if I'd be cool or not.

I came into our first hall meeting, sat the guys down, and explained the deal. I told them I was here to be their friend, not their dad. I told them it was their job to take care of themselves, and each other. When it came to alcohol, I told them that, "of course, state law says you can't drink." They all laughed; so did I. And then I said what my brother's RA said, "When it comes to alcohol on my hall, if I can't see it, it's not there." You would have thought that I just told a bunch of first graders that they were going to an amusement park instead of school for the next week. Mayhem ensued. They loved me. It worked out just as I planned!

They didn't wait long to take full advantage of the policy. That night there were about 50 people crammed into two rooms on my hall. I think there were two kegs in there too, but I stayed in my room and away from the stairwell, so I didn't see anything coming in. That pretty much continued most of the year. In the beginning I thought it was cool. But then the housekeeper started letting me know that she was getting tired of cleaning up our dirty bathroom—you can only imagine what it looked like. My boss kept harping on me like I wasn't doing my job correctly. I tried to explain to him that I knew my guys were fine and they just liked to have a little fun. Yeah, a couple guys went to the hospital that one night, but it was the last day of classes for their first semester in college; they'll have great stories to tell their kids.

Then during the second semester, I got put on probation as an RA. I thought it was total crap. I was told that if I didn't confront the next party on my floor that I'd be fired. So, the next weekend, when the party started, I reluctantly went down the hall to write the guys up so I could keep my job. I figured they'd understand, after all, I needed the job to stay in school. As I walked down the hall, one of the guys walked out of the room with a can of beer, and quickly put it under his shirt. "You can't see this," he yelled. I knocked on the door. One of my guys opened it and told me to go away—that I didn't want to see what was going on inside the room. After awhile, the two guys who lived there came to the door and said, "Come on Scott, go back to your room, or just get out of here, what you don't see isn't here, right?"

I told them to ask their guests to leave and wrote them up. I've never seen anyone so pissed.

For the rest of the year, they called me every name in the book. "Traitor" and "two-face" are the only ones I can say in polite company. They never spoke to me, much less hung out in my room, again. I was crushed.

The rest of the year, I felt like Saddam Hussein living in a retirement home for U.S. veterans. As I write this letter, it is the week after I graduated from college. I heard that one of my residents from that year is now in rehab. It turns out that he drank so much every night that he became an alcoholic. A few others got arrested for DUI and disorderly contact in the town next to us—they never got in trouble at school, but now they have arrest records keeping them out of medical school and good jobs. And for the guys who went to the hospital, their parents sure were pissed when they got the hospital bills. They had to work all summer to pay their parents back.

Getting Some Advice

At the end of the year, I had my annual evaluation with my boss. Needless to say it didn't go too well. On the other hand, I was able to reflect on my decisions, and what I should have done instead. My boss reminded me that one of the first things he said to us at the beginning of the year was, "It is much easier to begin the year by being strict on policy than it is to start off relaxed and try to reassert control later." At the time, I thought he was being too uptight. When we talked about it in my evaluation, it made a lot more sense. I learned that while I was trying to be cool, I was putting a lot of people in jeopardy in the process, and really wasn't helping anyone.

A Second Try

The next year, surprisingly enough, I was allowed to be an RA again. I'm sure if we were at a school where getting an RA position is competitive that I would not have been rehired, but they have a tough time getting people to do the job here, and I was willing to promise to do my job a lot better this time around—especially with regard to enforcing policy. This time, I did things a lot differently. I explained policy to my residents, my role in it, and their role in living up to it. The first time someone brought alcohol on the floor, I confronted it, documented it, and asked him not to put me in that position again. He felt bad about it, and we ended up getting along really well after a few days. The rest of the year wasn't perfect, of course, but I had a much better year. I wish I had handled things that way my first year as an RA.

Lessons Learned

So in the end, I learned a tough lesson through experience. It may seem like a good policy to say, "What I can't see, isn't there." In the beginning, your residents may even think you're the greatest RA ever. But in the end, at least in my case, my residents ended up hating me, and many of them suffered a lot of consequences that they might not otherwise have had to go through if I had just kept them under control a little bit more. Should RAs be junior varsity police officers? Well, no. But we do have an important role in policy enforcement, and if we don't do it, a lot of people can get hurt in the process. I hope you learn something from my experience. Good luck!

Keep it real,
Scott

Discussion Questions

1. Why do you think Scott told his residents "If I can't see it, it isn't there?"
2. Besides what actually happened, what might have been other consequences of his saying this?
3. What are some responsible ways of explaining policy to residents?
4. What are some responsible ways of confronting policy violations?

5. How can you tell if you have a resident who might have a drinking problem?

6. What are some ways that you can talk with that resident to assist him or her in making good future choices?

7. Besides what Scott did during his "second try," what are some other ways he could have addressed policy in an appropriate fashion?

8. What are the most helpful things you learned from this scenario?

9. How will you act differently as an RA, based on this new knowledge?

Resources

Effective Confrontation
http://www.reslife.net/html/tools_0804a.html
Difficult Situations: A Model for Handling Conduct Violations
http://www.reslife.net/html/tools_0901a.html
Confrontation—It's All About the Attitude
http://www.reslife.net/html/tools_0804a.html
Confronting Negative Behavior
http://www.residentassistant.com/advice/negbehavior.htm

Tips on Fair Enforcement

1. When you are aware of it, confront it.

2. Do it the same way, all the time.

3. Let residents know it is them, not you, who are responsible for the situation.

4. Avoid the trap of avoiding policy enforcement; it will come back to haunt you!

5. Remember that you may be saving someone from a whole lot of trouble down the road if you confront them now.

19

ENJOYING POLICY
ENFORCEMENT TOO MUCH

Dear Fellow RA,

My name is Christopher and I'm a second year RA at Rolling Mountains University. I came to RMU because they have a great criminal justice program. It also has good programs in engineering and physics, with a decent business school as well. About 25,000 students go here, mostly from within the state and surrounding region.

Both my father and my grandfather are cops, and I want to be one, too. I figured that while I'm here majoring in criminal justice, that I'd be an RA too to get some good practice in busting people. My freshman year was awful. Everyone on my floor drank beer all the time (even at 2 p.m. in the afternoon), and they made all kinds of racket at all hours of the day and night. I decided two weeks into my freshman year that I'd be an RA during my sophomore year and would make sure that no one got out of line.

The Situation

Move in day went according to plan. I gave all my residents their keys, told them we'd have a meeting at 6 p.m. sharp, that they should spend the afternoon setting up their room, and that they should be sure to go to the dining hall early for dinner so that they weren't late for my meeting. I marched them over to dinner together, and had each sit at a table I preselected for its proximity to the exterior door so that we could get out in time for our meeting at 6 p.m. Having already set up chairs in the lounge all facing forward, I told my guys to file in and I'd be there in a minute. Once they all got in there, I put on my army fatigues and came in with my grandfather's dagger that he wrestled away from a German soldier in World War II. It is an exquisite piece of weaponry. I walked to the front of the room, stood behind the wooden table in front of me, and with an exaggerated circular hand motion, plunged that dagger into the table so hard that it stuck down in there almost an inch. I then proclaimed "My hall!" My residents were so scared that they almost lost bladder control. I had established control. It was great!

Then on the first weekend night at 7:30 p.m., one of the guys on my floor had his music on so loud I could make out the lyrics to the song if I stood 5 feet from his closed door and listened carefully. So, I went by the book and busted him. My first bust went just like it was supposed to go. He seemed both confused and annoyed. I really showed him who was boss. Later that night I got a tip that one of my boys had a beer in his room. Given that this was my first AV (alcohol violation), I called for back up. I had one of my fellow staff members stand outside the resident's window in case the resident decided to throw the evidence out the window. I placed another staff member on the opposite side of the quad where he could look in the window of the resident's room so that we could document what he did when I knocked on the door, and a third RA behind me for back-up muscle (the intimidation factor). I banged on the door and said, "RA, open this door in three seconds or I will key in with the master." He opened the door, I grabbed him and the beer, had him dump it out in the bathroom after passing by all of the rest of the guys on the hall on the way, and told him he'd be meeting with the Dean on Monday, and maybe the police and district attorney, too.

So with my first alcohol bust behind me, I went to bed satisfied. I slept like a baby. When I woke up the next morning, I looked over toward the door, and saw a puddle. Not being sure what it was, I got up and realized when I got closer that it was urine. I opened my door, and the big puddle of urine extended well outside my door. There wasn't much time for me to look at it, because a pile of about 100 beer cans was balanced precariously above my door, rigged to fall on my head once I walked out into the hallway. Those engineering majors, they think they can rig up any kind of contraption! Once the beer cans all fell down, I looked on the wall across from my room and saw spray-painted on the wall my name, along with an extensive list of insults. What had I done to deserve this?

Getting Some Advice

My Area Coordinator was a bit of a wimp, so I decided to call my cousin for advice. He had been an RA five years back. I told him how my first day went from the dinner on. He kept saying "Oh! Ouch! Yikes!" the whole time I told the story. I thought he was proud of me; instead, he was pained by my story. Once I finished, he told me that no one deserves to have their residents pee on their floor and rig up a beer can bomb on their head. However, he suggested that I could have started off with them better. After a long talk, I realized that I was not running a prison—I was leading a floor of guys in college. I realized that if you enjoy busting people too much, it doesn't do anybody much good. I also realized that I needed to be human to my residents, not a policy enforcement robot. Yes, there were rules. Yes, they needed to live by them. However, if I set myself up in the way I did, I'd never earn their confidence and respect to help them through their first year of college.

A Second Chance

Fortunately, my residents were cool enough to listen to me when I asked them to come to a meeting to talk things over. I explained where I had been coming from, that I'd still enforce the rules, but that I now saw how overboard I'd been. By the end of the meeting, we were laughing about it, and I was laughing at myself. The rest of the year went a lot better.

Lessons Learned

More than anything I learned through my RA experience that there is a real problem if you enjoy policy enforcement too much. We are not junior varsity policemen. We are RAs. Policy enforcement is a big part of the job. However, if our residents think we are constantly looking for them to slip up, it creates an unhealthy environment on the floor. When it comes to policy enforcement, I learned that consistency is important—overzealous seeking of rule breakers is not. I hope you learn from my experience. Have a great year.

Sincerely,
Christopher

Discussion Questions

1. Where do you draw the line between enforcing policy by the book and going overboard?
2. What were some other ways Christopher could have handled his discipline role?
3. Is being an RA good training for being a police officer? Why or why not?
4. What are your thoughts about how the various residents responded to Christopher throughout this case?
5. How many of you are nervous about enforcing policy?
6. What are some issues you still need to discuss to feel more comfortable with this role?
7. What are the most helpful things you learned from this scenario?
8. How will you act differently as an RA, based on this new knowledge?

Resources

Effective Confrontation
http://www.reslife.net/html/tools_0804a.html
Difficult Situations: A Model for Handling Conduct Violations
http://www.reslife.net/html/tools_0901a.html
Being on Duty
http://www.residentassistant.com/advice/onduty.htm

Tips on not Enjoying Policy Enforcement

1. The quickest way to antagonize your residents is to show signs that you enjoy policy enforcement.
2. Remember you are not a junior varsity police officer; you are the leader of a community.
3. If you find you are enjoying policy enforcement, see a counselor to find out why.
4. Student misbehavior hurts everyone; confronting it is your job, but should not your joy.
5. Remember that much of policy enforcement is about educating residents to make better decisions.

20

ENFORCING POLICY SELECTIVELY

How to Really Annoy Your Residents

Dear Fellow RA,

Hi! My name is Linda. I go to Taylor University, home of the Fighting Foxes! We are located on the West Coast, near the beach. Lots of people come here for the great education they can get at Taylor; more people come here because we're near the beach and you can always find a good party. Being an RA is tough, especially in the upper-class halls where residents expect to get away with a lot. Last year when I was an RA for an upper-class floor, I had a really rocky start. Luckily enough, once I sorted everything out, it was smooth as the powdered sand on our beaches!

The Situation

I started the year off well, greeted all my residents, and had everyone gather on the beach for a cookout the first night. I was really surprised that everyone came, given that most of them had friends they wanted to see from last year. But, it was a free dinner and they still had time to go out afterward, so I guess they thought it was worth their time. I was really excited to see some of my friends from my first year who were living on my floor; I knew it would be just great having my friends as my residents! Or so I thought.

The first weekend, my friends had a party on the floor and invited practically everyone from our first-year dorm from last year. I didn't hear about it, until I heard it (literally). One of the guys from our hall the year before stopped by my room and thanked me for being so cool about the party. I didn't know what to do, so to avoid looking like I wasn't doing my job, I just left the building and went to a movie with one of my sorority sisters. I came back later that night and the hallway and hall bathroom were really trashed. This was going to be a long year.

The next weekend I was on duty, and a different group of residents on my floor were having a party. While I was on my rounds, I walked by their door, noticed the strong odor of alcohol, and confronted the party. Rosita answered the door, looked at me, looked back at her friends and said, "It's just Linda, we're cool." I asked Rosita to come out into the hallway, confirmed that there was underage drinking taking place, and asked her to clear out the party. She asked if I was joking. I confirmed that I was not joking. She had a fit. She accused me of busting their party just because most of them were Hispanic, and said that it was obvious I was a flaming racist because I hadn't busted the White women who had a party last weekend. She slammed the door in my face and yelled, "Everybody, you gotta go, my RA is a racist and she's busting us." I felt like I had the wind knocked out of me. Do you know that feeling deep in your gut like your guts just spilled out on the floor leaving a gaping hole inside you? Well, that is exactly how I felt at that moment.

Getting Some Advice

When I went to my Area Coordinator's office to turn in the incident report, I burst into tears. I told her everything about the party the first weekend, my leaving the hall, the party while I was on duty, being accused of racism, basically everything. My AC was really understanding about where I was coming from. She helped me to see how being inconsistent in policy enforcement can really hurt my relationships with all of my residents. I guess I had to learn that the hard way. And wow, was it hard. I didn't think things would ever get better.

A Second Chance

Everyone on the floor heard about what happened, and wouldn't talk to me for a few days. After things calmed down, I asked everyone to come to a floor meeting. To my surprise, they all came. I told the truth about all the decisions I had made, why I made them, how I recognized it when I was wrong, and asked them to forgive me. I also made it clear that I could not turn the other way, for anyone, if policy was violated. They could tell I was sincerely sorry, and to their great credit, they forgave me. The rest of the year went a lot better. In fact, they respected me at that point so much that they didn't put me in the position where I'd have to confront them about the alcohol policy. I wish I had started the year off that way, but better late than never.

Lessons Learned

Above all, I learned why they tell us as RAs to be consistent with policy enforcement. While you may think that it is OK to let a policy violation slide when a friend slips up, you have to think not only about them, and you, but also about your other residents and how your inconsistency can be perceived. If you let one violation slide, you set yourself up for a very difficult year. I learned that it is just not worth it. Consistency is the key to a successful year. I hope you learn from my experience. Have a great year!

Ciao,

Linda

Discussion Questions

1. Is it tempting to enforce policy one way with residents you know or like better than those you don't? Why?
2. Did Linda think she was doing a good thing by leaving the building when her residents were having a party? Was it a good thing? Why?
3. How much do you think residents notice about what the RA does and does not do when a policy violation is obvious?
4. Were the Latina residents justified in calling Linda a racist? Why or why not?
5. As far as you can tell, was Linda motivated by racism?

6. In what way could her actions have been interpreted as racist?

7. Why is it important for policy to be enforced consistently?

8. What are the most helpful things you learned from this scenario?

9. How will you act differently as an RA, based on this new knowledge?

Resources

Effective Confrontation
http://www.reslife.net/html/tools_0804a.html
Difficult Situations: A Model for Handling Conduct Violations
http://www.reslife.net/html/tools_0901a.html

Tips on Consistency

1. The most important time to enforce policy is the first time you see a violation!

2. Be sure to treat everyone the same way, all of the time.

3. Think about exactly what you will say before you go into a confrontation, so you won't stumble for words when under pressure.

4. Remind yourself that you act with integrity when you tell your supervisors and residents that you will enforce policy.

5. Policy enforcement is just one part of building community.

21

Ignoring Escalating Domestic Violence

Dear Fellow RA,

Hi there! My name is Susan, and I'm a senior at Aikins University. Aikins is a pretty small school on the East Coast. We only have about 5,000 undergraduates, and we're serious about academics. Our entire city is a historical place, and there's always a lot to learn both on and off campus. Most students here go on to get graduate degrees. I just love being an RA. Somehow I've managed to maintain a 3.9 GPA, my position as head cheerleader, and president of my sorority while being an RA. Let me tell you, that takes a lot of work! As an RA for two years now, and I've learned a lot. I thought I had seen just about everything, until a couple of months ago. Then I got caught up in a situation I never would have expected.

The Situation

Move-in was great, and because most of the women on my hall were juniors and seniors, everyone was pretty independent. Everything was fine until a few weeks before winter break. One of my residents, Mandy, seemed a little distant and stressed, but that was to be expected with final exams and all. Everyone was kind of tense. One evening, as I was doing rounds, I heard a loud voice coming from Mandy's room. I paused by her door and realized that the voice belonged to Mandy's boyfriend, Mike. I had seen them together around campus, and they usually seemed pretty happy. That night, though, Mike was screaming and I thought I heard Mandy crying. I wanted to knock and tell them to quiet down, but I figured it wasn't my business. Couples fight sometimes, right? So I just finished my rounds and hoped it would blow over soon.

Over the next few days, things seemed to get worse. Mandy wouldn't talk to anyone, was crying all the time, and I heard from a couple other residents that they saw Mike yelling and grabbing Mandy in the lounge. I told them that Mike always seemed nice enough, and it was probably a misunderstanding. But I started feeling pretty uneasy. So I went to Mandy and let her know that other residents heard the arguing. I suggested that if things were so bad maybe she and Mike should go their separate ways. Mandy just looked at me and said Mike was "under a lot of pressure" and everything would be okay soon. I told her to make sure it was, and I left. Huge mistake. Huge.

The next day, there was a knock on my door, and there was Mandy between two police officers. Her eye was swollen and bruised, and it was obvious that she had been crying…again. It seemed that Mandy and Mike had gotten into another argument and when Mandy started to leave, Mike hit her. She tried to get away, but Mike followed her and attacked her in a local store. Thankfully, someone called the police before Mandy got really hurt. Mike was arrested, and the police brought Mandy home.

Getting Some Advice

Of course, I had to inform my Resident Director, who had to make a report to Residence Life. My RD told me I should speak with Dr. Richards, the Staff Psychologist and Outreach Coordinator at the Counseling Center, to learn more about abusive relationships. Dr. Richards told me that domestic violence is a pattern of behavior that is used to gain or maintain power and control over an intimate partner, and it is more common in young adults than many people realize. She also taught me that you may be in an abusive relationship if your partner calls you names, insults, or continually criticizes you; is jealous of outside relationships or acts possessive; tries to isolate you from family and friends; monitors where you go, who you call, and who you spend time with; threatens to hurt you; humiliates you; damages property when angry; pushes, slaps, bites, kicks, or chokes you; has trapped you or kept you from leaving; or uses physical force in sexual situations.

When I thought about it, I could see some of the signs in Mandy's relationship. Mike's behavior was aggressive and threatening, and it was obvious that he tried to intimidate her. Dr. Richards also told me that many victims will deny the abuse because they're afraid, embarrassed, or they feel that they deserve it. A lot of times they'll even make excuses for the abuser. I thought about Mandy telling me how much pressure Mike was under when I confronted her about the arguments, and I felt sick. I couldn't believe how blind I had been.

A Second Chance

Naturally, I couldn't undo what had already been done, but I did have another conversation with Mandy. I apologized for not recognizing that she was in trouble, and for not asking if she needed help. I asked her if there was anything I could do for her. Mandy told me that she had to file charges against Mike and she wanted to file a restraining order as well, so she could use some support in doing that. She said she was really embarrassed that she let the situation get so out of hand, and she thought she didn't have anyone to turn to because she barely spoke to her friends anymore. I let her know that there were a lot of people who cared about her, and that she had support from me, the other residents, and all of her other friends. I also suggested that she visit the Counseling Center and speak with someone to help resolve her feelings and fears.

Lessons Learned

I realize that I may not always be able to tell if someone is a victim of domestic violence, but I should be more active about getting involved if I suspect that someone is being intimidated or threatened. Hopefully, I won't have to deal with this issue again, but if I do I'll be more prepared. More than anything I learned through my conversation with the counselor in the counseling center about some of the signs to watch for in an abusive relationship. Being an RA showed me that so much is going on with our residents. We might think that they lead perfect lives; but so many of them hide hurt just underneath the surface. Part of our job is to recognize that hurt, and try to help them deal with it. In the end, their life is their responsibility. But it is our responsibility to do what we can to help them live and learn in a safe community. I hope you learned from my experience. Have a great year!

See ya!
Susan

Discussion Questions

1. When did Susan have the chance to intervene on Mandy's behalf, and when did she not?
2. Why didn't Susan speak to Mandy and Mike about their arguments?
3. What actions could Susan have taken instead?
4. How can you recognize that a resident may be a victim of domestic violence?
5. Would you be comfortable talking with a resident that you believe is being abused? Why or why not?
6. What are the most helpful things you learned from this scenario?
7. How will you act differently as an RA, based on this new knowledge?

Resources

The Family Violence Prevention Fund
http://endabuse.org/
Women's Law
http://www.womenslaw.org/
Violence Against Women Online Resources
http://www.vaw.umn.edu/library/
The National Domestic Violence Hotline
http://www.ndvh.org/
National Online Resource Center on Violence Against Women
http://www.vawnet.org/
National Coalition Against Domestic Violence
http://www.ncadv.org/

Tips on Domestic Violence

1. Domestic violence is not "none of your business!"
2. Remember we always intervene if our residents' safety is at risk.
3. "Low level" violence can escalate quickly; intervene as soon as you suspect domestic violence.
4. Always refer the survivor to a counselor.
5. As with all serious incidents, tell your supervisor immediately.

22

ASSUMING A RESIDENT WHO COMES HOME DRUNK FREQUENTLY CAN HANDLE THEIR ALCOHOL

Dear Fellow RA,

My name is Jason. It feels weird writing you a letter as a "fellow RA," basically because I'm not an RA anymore. I lost my job as an RA (I was fired). At the time, I thought it was a load of b.s., but thinking about it now that it is a year later, I can kind of see why I was let go. As I write this letter, I'm about to graduate from Thomasville University. We have about 15,000 students and are known for our high quality academic program. And we know how to party, too.

I became an RA my sophomore year. I drank a lot my freshman year, mostly at rush events at different fraternities and also back in the dorm. I didn't end up pledging anywhere. I thought I'd get a bid from a couple houses but it didn't work out. No big deal though. During my sophomore year, my hall was "that hall." Do you know what I mean? Things were always happening on my hall—it was the social center of the first-year residential area. Everyone would come over to pre-game before they went out to parties. My residents drank a lot, but for the most part, they were pretty smart about it, at least I thought so. The Residence Life Office used to tell us all the time that we had to write kids up for drinking; I didn't really see the need unless they really had a drinking problem. Besides, I thought I knew my guys better than anyone else did. They had a couple parties that were busted by other RAs. My

Resident Director got kind of annoyed when he found out that I was on the floor when some of the parties happened and did nothing about it. After that happened a couple times, he put me on probation; no big deal though. My residents really appreciated me taking the heat for them.

The Situation

There was this one kid on my hall, Nathan, who had the least experience drinking in high school and tried to make up for it here at TU. One night he came home a little drunk and was staggering down the hallway. It seems to me that when he staggers around that isn't necessarily a sign that he is really, really drunk, it is just his body's reaction to alcohol. Well anyway, he went into his room and passed out. Awhile later, his roommate and other guys on the hall went in to mess with him and wrote stuff all over his forehead, arms, and chest. It was pretty funny, but I told them to stop and just let him sleep it off in peace. A few hours later, his roommate came to get me. I went to the room and saw a pile of vomit with blood in it next to Nathan. He wasn't moving. We took him to the bathroom, and he started moving a little and threw up some more. Then, what really ended up getting me in trouble later was that we put him back in bed to sleep it off. After a few more hours, Nathan's roommate came to get me again. He said he wasn't sure if Nathan was breathing. It turns out, he was breathing, but it was really shallow. One of the guys on the floor called 911, and Nathan went to the hospital. It turns out his blood alcohol content level was 38. He had almost died.

Getting Some Advice

Honestly, the "advice" I got in this situation was that I didn't have the instincts to be an RA who could keep my residents safe. At the time, I was really annoyed. I thought I was doing everything I should, it turns out, I was really putting my residents at risk. So, that weekend was my last as an RA.

A Second Chance

While I didn't get a second chance to be an RA, I did get a second chance to have a good college experience. I got involved in the campus newspaper and joined the club lacrosse team. I saw Nathan a few days ago. He had to take the semester off to go into rehab again. I couldn't help but think that if I had handled my RA role differently, that he would have turned out differently. I say this so that you might live my second chance for me.

Lessons Learned

It can be tempting to be cool, just let things slide, and not let administrators know when your residents are getting drunk. What I learned is that the rules are there to protect the health and safety of students, first and foremost. If I had done my job, Nathan's life might have turned out a lot differently. While I doubt I could have been the hard-ass they wanted me to be, I could have at least worked with my supervisors to figure out how to best support my residents and their health. So when you see your residents getting drunk, or you see them stumbling down the hallway, be the one to step in and make sure they are OK. If you are not sure, always, always, get help right away. Don't take the chance that it could be too late for them, and for you. I hope you learn from my experience. Have a great year!

Peace out,
Jason

Discussion Questions

1. Why do you think Jason was hesitant to enforce policy?
2. Does it sound like being an RA was a good choice for Jason?
3. What, specifically, would you do differently from Jason?
4. In what ways was Jason putting his residents at risk?
5. How can you tell that it is time to call 911 for a resident who has been drinking?
6. When should you document a student for drinking alcohol?

7. What are the policies of your school for when you should document an incident? Call a professional staff member at home or on call? Call 911?

8. What are the most helpful things you learned from this scenario?

9. How will you act differently as an RA, based on this new knowledge?

Resources

Alcohol Poisoning
http://www.campusblues.com/alc5.asp
Substance Abuse and Traumatic Brain Injury in College Students
http://www.reslife.net/html/tools_0103b.html
BRAD—Be Responsible About Drinking
http://www.brad21.org/
FAQ—What is Alcoholism?
http://www.campusblues.com/alc1.asp
National Institute on Alcohol Abuse and Alcoholism
http://www.niaaa.nih.gov/
Bacchus & Gamma Peer Education Network
http://www.bacchusgamma.org/
College Drinking—Changing the Culture
http://www.collegedrinkingprevention.gov/

Tips on Alcohol

1. Even if you see the same resident intoxicated with frequency, it only takes one time to die from alcohol poisoning.

2. Patterns of drunkenness are danger signals for alcoholism.

3. A resident may say he has only had a few drinks, but in reality, depending on who mixed them, how big the glass was, how much they had to eat, it can affect each person differently.

4. Never take a risk; when in doubt, get them to the emergency room!

5. You can't always tell from looking at someone how much they've had to drink. Don't risk being wrong.

23

ASSUMING THAT ALL STUDENTS WHO APPEAR INTOXICATED WERE DRINKING ALCOHOL AND NOT USING OTHER DRUGS

Dear Fellow RA,

Hi. My name is Claire. I just finished my first year as an R.A. at Franasiak University. Most of the students at our school went to private high schools. We have about 10,000 students, most of whom either go into business, or go to law or medical school after graduation. As a private university in the Southeast, we've been around a long time and have lots of traditions. Being an RA this year has really opened my eyes to worlds I didn't even know existed here at Franasiak.

The Situation

I'm used to residents drinking alcohol. It's the core component of most of the socializing that happens here, like most schools. Personally, I don't think it's a big deal, as long as it doesn't get too out of control. I keep a lid on things in my hall. The guys upstairs party a lot, but mostly keep it under control. The women on my hall definitely like to party, but mostly they don't pre-party on the floor and keep most of their drinking to parties outside the hall. Most weekends, I have at least a few residents who come home drunk—some weekends more than others and, of course, some residents more than others. My Area Director told us to write an incident report every time we witness a resident whom we believe is intoxicated. Honestly, when my AD said that during training, I thought she must be completely out of her mind. I'd run through a ream of paper during the first month. So I only wrote up incident reports when my residents really got out of hand—threw up in the hallway, woke everyone up at 4 a.m., had a loud party in their room, stuff like that.

Two of my residents, Rachel and Lisa, were two who came home every weekend acting drunk. After awhile, they didn't really attract my attention because they acted that way so frequently. Well, it turns out, they weren't drunk, they were high. No, they weren't just high on marijuana as you might think, but high on Ecstasy. It seems that they didn't want to gain weight from drinking alcohol, and didn't want the munchies that you get from pot, so their drug of choice was Ecstasy. When I heard a rumor that they were using E, I was just shocked. I knew some people here tried drugs, but I never thought any of my residents would—they were too smart.

Getting Some Advice

While I should have gone to my Area Director, I decided to talk with my health education professor, and asked about some of the symptoms of using E. In talking with Professor Modma, I realized that they had shown several signs of use. For example, sometimes they clenched their teeth funny, seemed to have blurred vision, appeared faint, and had either the chills or were sweating a lot. They would also touch each other and anyone they passed in the hallway excessively; not in a sexual way per se but just a touchy way—I thought they were just being drunk and friendly.

How did I find out for sure they were using? Well, second semester, Rachel didn't come back to school. Instead, she was involuntarily checked into drug rehab by her parents. My AD asked me if I ever noticed anything peculiar about her. Once I filled her in, everything fit together. I also realized I had made a huge mistake in not documenting her odd behavior before. I guess I was both naïve and thought I knew better than my AD. I really wish I had done something differently.

A Second Chance

Rachel was clearly a lot worse off than Lisa, but Lisa still had a problem. I was able to have a good conversation with Lisa about Rachel not coming back, and how drugs were affecting Lisa's own life. Much to my surprise, the fact that Rachel was in rehab really shook Lisa up. She started crying and was really afraid. At that point, I was able to convince Lisa to start going to Narcotics Anonymous meetings, and start seeing our drug and alcohol counselor in the counseling center on campus. I'm happy to say that by the end of the semester, despite one slip up, Lisa has made a lot of progress and has been sober now for two months. Over the summer she agreed to go to NA meetings and get a counselor back home. Hopefully, she'll be better in the long run, though I know that some of the effects of the drugs may stay with her for quite some time.

Lessons Learned

Wow, did I learn a lot from this experience. First, even when you disagree with your Area Director, there is probably a really good reason why they ask you to do things as they tell you. Second, not every resident who appears drunk is using alcohol; there are a lot of other things that could be in their system. Part of the reason we document residents is to get them in with a professional who can assess how the resident is doing. Third, I will never again be so lackadaisical about my residents coming home intoxicated. No matter how they got that way, it can be dangerous to themselves and possibly others. I hope you learned from my experience. Have a great year!

Sincerely yours,
Claire

Discussion Questions

1. Why do you think Claire was reluctant to document every situation on her hall that she was supposed to write up?
2. To what extent do you feel the same way that Claire did in the beginning?

3. Would it have occurred to you that residents were using drugs?

4. In what ways should our response be the same to residents using drugs as it is to residents using alcohol?

5. In what ways should our response be different for residents using drugs compared to residents using alcohol?

6. Do you think drug use is an issue on your campus? Why or why not?

7. What are the most helpful things you learned from this scenario?

8. How will you act differently as an RA, based on this new knowledge?

Resources

Information on Club Drugs
http://www.clubdrugs.org/
Information on Marijuana
http://www.campusblues.com/drugs8.asp
The Higher Ed. Center for Alcohol and Other Drug Abuse and Violence Prevention
http://www.edc.org/hec/
Narcotics Anonymous
http://www.na.org
Cocaine Anonymous
http://www.ca.org

Tips on Recognizing Drug Use

1. Not all people who appear drunk are using alcohol.

2. Familiarize yourself with the behaviors of people who use drugs.

3. A substantial number of college students use marijuana, Ecstasy, cocaine, and other drugs. Learn about them!

4. A person who is high can easily overdose as the drugs continue to be processed in their system. Get them medical attention!

5. If you see drugs, call the police.

PART 5

HELPING STUDENTS WITH PSYCHOLOGICAL DIFFICULTIES

CHAPTER 24 PROMISING A RESIDENT YOU WON'T TELL ANYONE WHAT YOU ARE ABOUT TO BE TOLD

CHAPTER 25 THINKING THAT THE SKINNY RESIDENT WHO KEEPS LOSING WEIGHT WILL BE OK

CHAPTER 26 DOING NOTHING ABOUT A STUDENT WHO MAKES A SUICIDAL COMMENT

CHAPTER 27 ASSUMING THAT THE STUDENT WHO MAKES SMALL CUTS ON DIFFERENT PARTS OF HER BODY WANTS TO KILL HERSELF

CHAPTER 28 HELPING A RESIDENT, AND YOUR FLOOR, SURVIVE A PANIC ATTACK

Handling situations where a student is mentally ill or has serious emotional problems can be among the toughest things an RA ever has to do. The stakes are very high—at times, life or death. Dealing with these situations, with the active support of your supervisor, is critically important. In chapter 24, we learn from Peggy's experience to never make a promise to keep something confidential without first knowing the nature of the information that will be shared with you. We learn through Lisa's experience in chapter 25 that eating disorders are very serious and should be treated as such. Next, April shows us how not taking a suicidal comment seriously can be a terrible mistake. Delia's experience in chapter 27 teaches us valuable lessons about "cutting" behavior. Finally, Arielle learns a lesson that we can all grow from about how to deal with someone having a panic attack.

24

Promising a Resident You Won't Tell Anyone what You Are About To Be Told

Dear Fellow RA,

Hi! My name is Peggy. I'm an RA at New England College for Women, home of the Mighty Mustangs! We just celebrated our 150th anniversary as a Women's College, and are proud of our heritage of educating some of the nation's most prominent women leaders. Here at NECW, we have a very active and vibrant residential community. Nearly 95% of our students live on campus in a traditional house system. Most residents live in the same house for all four years they are here, and often develop lifelong friendships with women in their house. I've been the house counselor (that's what we call RAs) in "Yingling House" for three years now. I lived here my first year, and had such a great experience with my house counselor, that I wanted to be the HC the next year. That plan worked out, and I've led our house ever since. It is tough to be graduating this year, but it's my time to move on and time for someone else to take up the reins of Yingling House.

The Situation

Women here, as I mentioned, form close bonds with each other. As the HC, I do a lot of supporting residents through the challenges and pitfalls of college. My door is always open, and many residents share their most intimate struggles and challenges with me. I think I should be given an honorary degree in psychology to go with the botany degree I'm getting this May just based on all the informal counseling I've done during the last three years! One of the women who stops by my room most frequently is June. June is an outgoing resident who is very popular in the house. One day during my sophomore year, June stopped by to see me. She and I were both residents of Yingling house the year before, so we knew each other well. One of the first things June said was, "OK, you've got to promise me you absolutely won't tell anyone what I'm about to tell you." She had a really serious and disturbed look on her face. I asked her why I needed to promise not to tell anyone. She simply said that I just needed to promise her not to tell anybody. So, I said OK and I promised her that I wouldn't tell anyone what she was about to tell me. June told me that she overheard a conversation between two other residents, Ann and Molly, in the bathroom. Molly was saying that her boyfriend Wayne had just dumped her and that she didn't know what she was going to do. In fact, Molly said she was so upset that she didn't know if she wanted to "go on anymore." Ann told her not to be ridiculous and to just get over Wayne, besides; Dominick from back home would go out with her in a heartbeat. June went on to say that later in the day, she talked to Molly. During that conversation Molly said she had skipped all her classes that week, was not sleeping well, and was thinking of trying cocaine for the first time that weekend. June wasn't sure what to say, so she just listened.

That's when June came to talk with me. June was concerned about Molly, but didn't want me to talk with Molly in person. Instead, June insisted that she be the one to talk with Molly, because Molly trusts her more. I could see her point, but felt a little uncomfortable about it. I decided that I would honor June's request—I told no one about our conversation, even the Director of Residence Life to whom I was supposed to report any such incident. I just gave June advice on how to talk to Molly and left it at that.

That weekend, Molly was carried home from a party by friends of hers, and plopped down on her bed where she passed out. It turns out she had a lot to drink and had snorted some cocaine, but no one was sure how much of either. She ended up in the hospital having her stomach pumped. The people partying with her just thought she had taken recreational drugs of some kind and would be fine. I don't know exactly what she took, but she was definitely not fine. Once in the hospital, they took good care of her and she recovered, but I felt really bad about what happened.

Getting Some Advice

On Monday morning, I went to talk with Dr. Mamie, the Director of Residence Life. I told her about everything that happened that week with June talking to me, me saying I wouldn't tell anyone what she said, etc. It was a hard conversation, because in the process I realized that by promising June I wouldn't tell anyone what she said, I was not only going against my job responsibilities but I was putting Molly at great risk for harm. Dr. Mamie put me on probation for my job, making it clear that I was never again to promise a resident confidentiality in the way that I had chosen to do. She could have fired me, but didn't. For that I was thankful.

A Second Chance

I was extremely fortunate to have a second chance in this situation. When I didn't fulfill my role as expected, my inaction could have led to a student's death. It doesn't get any more serious than that. The next time I had a resident come to me asking me to promise them not to tell anyone what they were about to say, I said, "I'll do my best to keep what you tell me in confidence, but if you say something about someone who might be a threat to themselves or to others, we may have to talk about who else I need to get some advice from." When I said this, my resident didn't like what she heard, but as I talked it through with her, she understood that it was in everyone's best interest.

Lessons Learned

I learned a lot from the incident with June and Molly. I learned not to promise a resident something without knowing what I'm promising them. I learned to follow the procedures I'd been given by my employer. I learned that sometimes going against a resident's request is what is best for them in the long run, even if our relationship suffers in the meantime. I also learned that when it comes to helping a resident who might harm herself, quick action and getting others involved right away is of paramount importance. I hope you learn from my experience. Have a great year!

Be well,

Peggy

Discussion Questions

1. Why do you think June asked Peggy to keep their conversation confidential?

2. What do you think were some of the reasons Peggy agreed not to tell anyone?

3. What were the results of Peggy not telling anyone?

4. What else could have resulted from Peggy not telling anyone?

5. What are some different approaches to explaining to residents about what we as staff can keep in confidence, what we can't keep in confidence, and why this is so?

6. How would you explain to residents what your role is with regard to keeping things confidential?

7. What are the most helpful things you learned from this scenario?

8. How will you act differently as an RA, based on this new knowledge?

Resources

Go Ask Alice! Emotional Health
http://www.goaskalice.columbia.edu/Cat4.html
Understanding Mental Disorders
http://www.reslife.net/html/tools_1101c.html

Tips on Dealing with Troubled Residents

1. Never promise a resident to keep a secret without knowing what you are promising.
2. The first sign that someone is going to hurt themselves is that they tell someone. Take all threats seriously!
3. Always seek immediate help if you are concerned that a resident may hurt himself or herself.
4. Talk with your supervisor before a problem really gets out of hand.
5. Check in with all of your residents regularly to see how they are doing.

25

THINKING THAT THE SKINNY RESIDENT WHO KEEPS LOSING WEIGHT WILL BE OK

Dear Fellow RA,

Hi, my name is Lisa. I'm an RA at Murry University, home of the Mighty Buffalo! MU is a big state school in the Rocky Mountains. Most people who come to MU were athletes in high school. We have a huge, famous workout facility on our campus and several nationally competitive athletic teams. Just about everyone here is either on an NCAA athletic team, a club team, or intramural team of some kind. Many of our students come from affluent families. About half of the women here have had debutante balls. Most everyone went to private high schools before coming here. I just finished my first year as an RA. Final exams were rough, because I was spending so much time seeing one of my residents in the hospital. Here's the story.

The Situation

From the knowledge I gained through RA training, I was able to notice that Kimberly had an eating disorder within the first few weeks of school. She was about five feet eight inches tall, weighed about 100 pounds, and had poor abdominal muscle tone despite a very demanding daily schedule of running and lifting weights. A few times I heard her throwing up in the bathroom. When I asked her about it, she said that she was having trouble getting used to the food in the cafeteria and that she was used to feeling sick after eating. She assured me it was no big deal. I figured it was really none of my business, so I ignored it.

As the year went on, Kimberly kept losing weight and continued to throw up frequently after meals. Finally, my Resident Director, Maureen, told me that some of Kimberly's friends came to meet with her to say they were worried about her. Maureen asked if I had noticed anything that concerned me about Kimberly.

Getting Some Advice

When I relayed all of the information to Maureen about everything I noticed, she was pretty upset that I hadn't told her before. I tried to explain that it was really no big deal and it was Kimberly's business. Maureen explained to me that people with eating disorders should not just be ignored because they can really end up very sick, or in some cases, even die from their condition. In fact, 10% of women who are hospitalized for an eating disorder end up dying from their disease. I had no idea it was that serious. Together, we devised a plan about how to proceed.

A Second Try

Maureen and I decided to meet with Kimberly together. I asked Kimberly if she'd be willing to go with me to see our Resident Director to talk about the food in the dining hall. Kimberly reluctantly agreed, but figured she'd have a chance to complain about what they served in the hopes that the food would get better. Maureen started the meeting by telling Kimberly that some of her friends came in the other day to say how worried they were about her and that they hoped Kimberly could learn more about how to take better care of herself. Kimberly was pretty defensive, but she listened. Maureen explained that she was there to help, not judge her decisions. She also explained that she did not have the expertise to diagnose an eating disorder, but that she did have the ability to recognize behavior that is destructive or disruptive to others, and that she wanted to help Kimberly find the right resources to stay as healthy as she could. I then explained that other residents had come to me concerned about how often she threw up, and a few were pretty angry that they had to use a bathroom that so frequently smelled like vomit. Maureen asked if Kimberly would be willing to see a nutritionist to talk about how to find food in the dining hall that she'd be more comfortable eating. She also asked Kimberly to make an appointment to see a counselor in our counseling center. Eventually, she reluctantly agreed to do both of these things.

It is a tough situation, because although Kimberly did what we asked, later in the year she ended up getting worse, passed out in the middle of the hall, and was rushed to the hospital. She wasn't able to take her exams, and her parents are taking her to an inpatient treatment facility in the hopes that she will get better. I hope some day she will. Next time I have a resident with an eating disorder, I'll be sure to be more proactive sooner in the year.

Lessons Learned

I'd have to say that the biggest thing I learned in my first year as an RA was not to overlook unhealthy behavior in my residents. What may seem like "just their business" is something that can not only affect others, but be dangerous to them. The other big lesson I learned from this was to discuss everything with my supervisor. There is a reason why we stay connected to professionals in residence life—many times they've dealt with these situations before and can be really helpful, aside from the fact that we really have to let them know what is going on given the contracts we sign for our job.

I hope you learned from my experience. Have a great year!

Yours truly,
Lisa

Discussion Questions

1. Why do you think Lisa didn't say anything to Kimberly early on?
2. What are some of the signs of someone who has an eating disorder?

3. What are some of the challenges of helping someone with an eating disorder?

4. Why is it important to be proactive in helping someone with disordered eating?

5. What are the most helpful things you learned from this scenario?

6. How will you act differently as an RA, based on this new knowledge?

Resources

Eating Disorders Anonymous
http://www.eatingdisordersanonymous.org/
Something Fishy—Web site on Eating Disorders
http://www.something-fishy.org/
Academy for Eating Disorders
http://www.aedweb.org/index.cfm
National Association of Anorexia Nervosa and Associated Disorders
http://www.anad.org
Go Ask Alice! Emotional Health
http://www.goaskalice.columbia.edu/Cat4.html
Understanding Mental Disorders
http://www.reslife.net/html/tools_1101c.html

Tips on Dealing with Eating Disorders

1. People with eating disorders are likely to be very defensive. Try to connect with them on a personal level.

2. Ten percent of people hospitalized with eating disorders end up dying from the disease. They are serious illnesses!

3. If you see the signs of a resident with an eating disorder, talk with your supervisor about ways to intervene quickly!

4. Schedule healthy eating workshops for your residents on your floor.

5. Talk with the dietician in your dining hall about resources to offer to your residents on healthy eating.

26

DOING NOTHING ABOUT A STUDENT WHO MAKES A SUICIDAL COMMENT

Dear Fellow RA,

My name is April. I go to Big State University (BSU). We are a large public school with 40,000 students, about 15,000 of whom live on campus. I'm now in my third year as an RA. Last year I was an RA in Bowman Hall—the residence hall for students in our honors program. As the only returner on staff, I played a major leadership role in the building—advising hall council, answering questions of the other RAs when our Resident Director wasn't around, that sort of thing. I've always loved being an RA, though it can be taxing at times. I pride myself on learning all my resident's names within an hour of their arrival on campus. Last year they gave me a pretty big group of residents—60 women, all of whom were students in the honors program. Half of them (one side of a two sided hall) were first-year women.

The year started off great. My first-year women were clicking together well and went to dinner at the dining hall every night as a group. The upper-class women were helping the first years get adjusted. There were three birthdays during the first week, so the floor organized a birthday party in the lounge to surprise the three residents with birthdays. A few of us worked all afternoon blowing up balloons, hanging streamers, and making a cake. The cake was a bit overdone and dry, but we all had fun anyway.

There was this one resident last year, Julie, who was, well, kind of a drama queen. There really is no other way to say it. Every day she'd come home with another story about why her life was harder than everyone else's. Do you know the type? When she had a bad day, and that was most days, everyone heard about it (literally). I tried to reach out to her, but she didn't seem to want my help. She just wanted to complain about her day, so I let her have her space.

The Situation

One day Julie came home and had another one of her tantrums. She threw her books down on her floor and screamed obscenities, ending with "it's not worth it anymore." I went down to see what was going on, and her roommate Alice said that Julie was just having one of her tantrums. I asked Alice how Julie was doing lately, and Alice said "Well she hasn't slept a lot lately, and I don't think she's eaten much in the last couple days, but that's just Julie—always doing something weird to get attention." I didn't think too much of it. While I was talking with Alice, Julie came back in the room. I asked her why she was upset. Julie just said, "Because this place sucks, life sucks, and I've had it with both." I asked her to clarify what she meant. She just stared at me and walked out of the room. Alice told me that Julie recently got some pills sent to her through the mail. Alice didn't know what they were, but she surely hoped they would calm Julie down.

I had to go off to class, so I left the building and got distracted with several other things going on. I figured I'd file an incident report the next day and talk it over with my RD at our next one-on-one the following week. One of these days we'd just have to get Julie to stop being such a drama queen and take better care of herself. Waiting to talk with my RD ended up being a bad decision.

I came back to the floor later that evening and everything was really tense. It felt like a combination of Sorority Rush and Final Exams. I knew something was wrong. I asked one of my residents what was up. She looked at me in disbelief and said, "Haven't you heard yet?" Just then, my RD came out of another resident's room and asked to talk with me in my room. Julie had tried to kill herself. I was devastated.

It turns out that she had a lot of stuff going on back home, and things weren't going much better here. I didn't know, but she tried to kill herself three times in high school. This time, she decided that if she was going to try, she would get the job done correctly. She ordered a bottle of pills from an online pharmacy—enough to kill an elephant, and certainly a person, within a few hours. After I had left to go to class earlier in the day, she was screaming down the hall, "No one around here cares about me anyway, even the RA doesn't care." Soon after, she took about 50 pills and began convulsing on the floor of the hall bathroom.

One of the residents found her, called 911, and thankfully they got to her in time. It took me about a year of therapy to convince myself that it wasn't my fault that she tried to kill herself. Still, there were things I could have done to better help her, and I should have acted more quickly.

Getting Some Advice

As part of my own therapy, I learned from my counselor in the counseling center that when someone makes an offhanded comment about life not being worth it, they probably mean it. It is far better to act on the side of caution than it is to hope things get better with time. I realized that I should have been keeping my RD better informed about Julie all along, and I should have called my RD or campus police when I saw that Julie was spinning out of control. I learned that some big warning signs are changes in eating or sleeping habits, depression, hopelessness, impulsivity, and having a means to end one's life. Now that I think about it, Julie showed all of those things, I just wasn't paying attention. I should have asked her more direct questions about how she was feeling, if she was thinking of harming herself, etc. I also should have kept my RD and other supervisors informed every step of the way.

A Second Chance

Luckily for me, and especially for Julie, there were people around with the presence of mind to call for help when she needed it most. Julie ended up dropping out of school and going home. From what I understand, home isn't much better a place for her to be than school, but at least she is still alive. This year I have a resident who reminds me a little bit of Julie. She has the same kind of attitude that Julie showed, and goes through the same "poor me" cycles on almost a daily basis. This time, I'm trying much harder to make sure she knows I'm part of her support system and I'm letting my new RD know how things are going. We were able to convince her to see a counselor on campus, and her new medication seems to be helping her cope.

Lessons Learned

The biggest lesson I learned as an RA was to never take a risk with someone who might be suicidal. Always err on the side of caution. Always tell your supervisor, or a counselor on call, if you have a resident who might be a danger to themselves or others. Take everything they say seriously, and act immediately if they make any comments at all about hurting themselves. I hope you learn from my experience. Have a great year!

Peace,
April

Discussion Questions

1. What are some possible ways to reach out to residents like Julie?
2. What are some of the decisions that April made that she should have done differently?
3. What were some signs that Julie needed help?
4. What are some other signs that a resident might be suicidal?
5. What is the policy on your campus about what to do when a student is suicidal?
6. What are the most helpful things you learned from this scenario?
7. How will you act differently as an RA, based on this new knowledge?

Resources

How to Deal with Suicidal Students
http://www.studentaffairs.com/onlinetraining/sample-suicidemodule.htm
Understanding and Preventing Suicide on Campus: A Case Study
http://www.collegepubs.com/ref/Suicide_Prevention.shtml
American Foundation for Suicide Prevention
http://www.afsp.org/
Go Ask Alice! Emotional Health
http://www.goaskalice.columbia.edu/Cat4.html
Understanding Mental Disorders
http://www.reslife.net/html/tools_1101c.html

Tips on Dealing with Suicidal Students

1. Always take seriously any mention a resident makes of hurting themselves or others. Get help immediately from a supervisor or the police.
2. The first sign that someone is going to hurt themselves is that they tell someone. Respond right away without delay!
3. Always seek immediate help if you are concerned that a resident may hurt himself or herself.
4. Talk with your supervisor before a problem really gets out of hand.
5. Check in with all of your residents regularly to see how they are doing.

27

ASSUMING THAT THE STUDENT WHO MAKES SMALL CUTS ON DIFFERENT PARTS OF HER BODY WANTS TO KILL HERSELF

Dear Fellow RA,

Hi! My name is Delia. I attend Stressed Out State University located in a town named Hypertension, in New England. We are a midsized public school where people get really uptight about classes, studying, activities, and just about everything. You should see this place around exam time. Scary! The weather is pretty cold up here compared to my hometown in the South! I've found that people at SOSU deal with stress much differently than they do down south. In one particular instance I had a resident who was behaving in a way I found bizarre, and it really freaked me out. I'm still a little uneasy about it, but I understand it better these days. So here's the deal…

The Situation

Michelle came from a home where she was the sixth of eight children. There was a lot of family pressure to be perfect and not much support when she didn't do a perfect job on everything. Michelle confided in me early on during the year that she felt a lot of anxiety, frustration, and anger toward her family and her life. They were very intolerant of anything but excellence. That seemed fairly normal, albeit not the case with everyone I know, it was normal for SOSU. However what struck me as odd was when she said that she sometimes got the sense that she was not even real—like she was a robot and her body and emotions were not connected. I wasn't sure what to do with that, so I asked my Resident Director. We were able to get Michelle to see a counselor at the counseling center, and they developed a good relationship. No RA should ever deal with a student like this alone!

Well, one day I came home from class and I saw Michelle sitting on her bed with a strange look on her face. As I looked closer, I realized that she had just used a razor blade to cut a two-inch long surface-level cut at the very top of her arm. I freaked out. There is no other way to say it. I just absolutely went berserk! I called 911 for the police and an ambulance to come get her. I told the operator that one of my residents had just tried to kill herself with a razor blade and they needed to get over here right away before she bled all over the place and died. I was so sure she was trying to kill herself! Michelle went to the hospital and was discharged soon thereafter, and got really peeved with me.

Getting Some Advice

The next day I went to the counseling center. When I spoke to Dr. Dante, she explained to me what "cutting" was. Cutting?!?! Not something I'd heard of in my hometown. It turns out that there are some people who experience a lot of anxiety, frustration, and anger who feel the need to punish themselves when they do something wrong. They often report that cutting themselves superficially becomes a relief; it is something that is real—better to feel real and alive than to feel nothing at all. It helps some people, usually women, feel in control and prove that they are alive. Most cutters will not kill themselves. That being said, I learned that it was good for me to want to get help for Michelle. Calling 911 was a good thing, but I didn't need to get so excited about it and say she was trying to kill herself.

A Second Chance

Finally after a month that seemed like an eternity, Michelle began to trust me again. She explained why she cuts herself sometimes. I explained how it can make me and other residents feel, and reinforced with her the importance of finding other ways to manage her stress. I think we both learned a lot from that discussion.

Lessons Learned

The biggest piece of advice I have for you as you start out your year on staff is to pay really close attention when they train you about students with psychological problems. One way or another, you are going to come across some behavior that you don't understand very well. It will help you out TONS if you learn about it beforehand, instead of freaking out like I did. Remember: don't be "the last to know" about your residents who are having trouble—always pass that information up your supervisory chain to be sure you are supporting your residents in the best way that you can. I hope you learned from my experience. Have a great year!

Later y'all,
Delia

Discussion Questions

1. How do you think you would have reacted if you saw Michelle cutting herself?
2. What do you think are the possible ways Delia could have reacted?
3. What would have been the best thing for Delia to do?
4. What are the protocols for you in your staff position if you come upon a situation like this?
5. Why do some people cut themselves in this way?
6. How do you personally react to this sort of thing? What more do you need to understand?
7. What are the most helpful things you learned from this scenario?
8. How will you act differently as an RA, based on this new knowledge?

Resources

What is Self-Mutilation?
http://www.coolnurse.com/self-injury.htm
SAFE (Self-Abuse Finally Ends) Alternatives
http://selfinjury.com/
ASHIC (American Self-Harm Information Clearinghouse)
http://selfinjury.org/
Go Ask Alice! Emotional Health
http://www.goaskalice.columbia.edu/Cat4.html
Understanding Mental Disorders
http://www.reslife.net/html/tools_1101c.html

Tips on Cutting

1. Not all "cutters" who make superficial cuts want to kill themselves.
2. Cutting is a characteristic of some mental illnesses and should be treated.
3. Don't decide yourself if your resident is a "cutter" or wants to kill themselves—get your supervisor involved!
4. Some cutters seek a mental or physical release through bleeding. It may seem bizarre to some, but natural to them personally.
5. Read up on the latest research on cutting.

28

Helping a Resident, and Your Floor, Survive a Panic Attack

Dear Fellow RA,

Hi, my name is Arielle. I got to McArdle Polytechnic Institute (MPI). Our school has about 10,000 students, about half of whom live on campus. As I write this, I'm in my second year as an RA. The biggest mistake I made last year as an RA was freaking out when one of my residents had what I now know was a panic attack. At the time I had no idea what the problem was. I thought she was drunk or just being obnoxious. Let me explain.

The Situation

Nancy was one of those residents who was just a little different from the other women on my hall. She was really moody, sometimes wanting to be all alone and at other times wanting to be in the middle of everything. One day I got back to the floor after class and Nancy ran by me, almost knocking me over. The first thing I did was yell at her to slow down and stop acting like a "raving lunatic." I came to regret using that phrase. She went into the stairwell, fell down the stairs, and started breathing really heavily. At that point, I called 911. I went after her in the stairwell and had no idea what to do. She got scared when I got near her; she didn't seem able to control her breathing and she was sweating all over the place. She also had a small cut on her arm from grazing by a railing with a jagged edge on it. Fortunately, the ambulance got there quickly. They determined that Nancy was having a panic attack. I had no idea what they meant, but after awhile she calmed down. She wanted to go back to her room and they let her go. Right about then I remembered how I reacted to her running down the hallway, and I felt pretty bad. I went to Nancy's door to talk with her about it, but she just closed the door in my face saying that she was fine and that there was no need for me to talk with a "raving lunatic" like her.

Getting Some Advice

The next day I went to the counseling center to talk with a psychologist about panic attacks. I asked her to explain to me what they are. I learned a whole lot! Together we pulled up information off of www. anxietypanic.com to look at what a panic attack is. We found out that the symptoms of a panic attack are a rapid heartbeat, trouble breathing, a feeling of terror that almost paralyzes the individual, a dizzy feeling sometimes accompanied by nausea or lightheadedness, sweating, shaking, trembling, choking, pain or tightness in the chest, feeling really hot or cold, tingling extremities, and sudden fear of death. I learned that panic attacks and related disorders are quite treatable, and nothing to fear. However, they should of course be taken seriously. Based on the psychologist's suggestion, I went back to Nancy and had another talk with her.

A Second Try

Nancy said she was really embarrassed about what happened on the floor the other day, but was still annoyed with me about how I treated her. I apologized profusely, and eventually she accepted my apology. Once I told her that I went to see a counselor about panic attacks, she was really happy that I thought enough to go get more information. Nancy said she wished that other people understood that she wasn't "crazy." I suggested that we invite the counselor to the floor to do a program about panic attacks. Nancy liked the idea, as it would demystify what happened. Nancy and I planned the program together with the psychologist and it went just great.

Lessons Learned

Seeing someone have a panic attack isn't an easy thing. I never thought that living through that experience would be the biggest thing I would learn during my RA experience. I learned a great deal about mental illness and how people cope with it. I learned that calling someone a "raving lunatic" is in poor taste. I learned how people who cope with mental illnesses are often very courageous people who are highly functional and committed to their education. The next time I see someone have a panic attack, I know I'll respond much differently, and won't be as uncomfortable myself with what is going on. Rather, I will do my best to help them ride it out and calm down. I hope you learned from my experience. Have a great year!

Au revoir!
Arielle

Discussion Questions

1. What are your thoughts about Arielle's first reaction to Nancy running down the hall?
2. What else could Arielle have done during the panic attack?
3. What should Arielle have done after the panic attack with her residents?
4. Are there things about mental illness that make you uncomfortable?
5. What else do you think you need to understand about people who have a mental illness to best support them?
6. What are the most helpful things you learned from this scenario?
7. How will you act differently as an RA, based on this new knowledge?

Resources

Anxiety Web site
http://www.anxietypanic.com

Identifying Anxiety Disorders
http://www.nimh.nih.gov/healthinformation/anxietymenu.cfm
Dealing with Panic Attacks
http://www.campusblues.com/panic.asp
Anxiety Disorders Association of America
http://www.adaa.org/
The Anxiety Community
http://www.anxietyhelp.org/

Tips on Panic Attacks

1. Panic attacks can come on suddenly for no apparent reason.
2. Try to help the person calm down.
3. Keep other residents and people away as much as possible.
4. Assure people that your resident will be OK, she or he just need some space.
5. Be sure to have them seek medical attention to rule out serious health problems.

PART 6

THINGS THAT
CAN SERIOUSLY
COMPROMISE
YOUR ROLE

CHAPTER 29 BEING CARELESS ABOUT SPENDING
UNIVERSITY MONEY

CHAPTER 30 DECIDING WHAT TO DO BASED ON WHAT
EVERYONE ELSE DOES

CHAPTER 31 DATING A RESIDENT

CHAPTER 32 DRINKING ALCOHOL WITH UNDERAGE RESIDENTS

CHAPTER 33 STAFF CONFLICT: DEALING WITH A SLACKING
STAFF MEMBER

CHAPTER 34 DEALING WITH PARENTS

There are lots of pitfalls that are easy to fall victim to during your experience as an RA. Some seem easy to avoid, while others are tantalizingly tempting—seemingly harmless on the surface and powerfully damaging in the end. Part 6 provides several scenarios from which to learn. In chapter 29 we learn about a great RA, Doug, who learns one of life's toughest lessons when he is dismissed for misspending university money. Next in chapter 30, we hear from Ryon, who falls into the trap of following the crowd rather than his conscience and his supervisor's expectations. Following that, we learn from Tamika in chapter 31 that dating a resident is a big mistake to avoid. In chapter 32 we learn about Ben's big blunder that earns him a dismissal from staff so quickly his head spun. Next we hear of Julia's frustration with a fellow staff member who was the consummate slacker; though Julia could have handled her part of this equation much better of course in chapter 33. Finally, in chapter 34, we learn from the experience of Liz about the importance of keeping our resident's confidences first and above the wishes of their parents—even when we might have outside contact with them.

29

Being Careless about Spending University Money

Dear Fellow RA,

Hi. I'm Doug and I go to a large state school in Texas, Hutter University. Here at H.U. we pride ourselves in our being a big school, with big teams, big buildings, and big personality. We also have big budgets in our Residence Life Office, which makes us rare. I'm a pretty laid back guy, not much gets to me. I got into a big mess last year when I was an RA. It actually got me fired. Luckily, I didn't face any legal charges, but those were possible believe it or not.

The Situation

It was the end of the fall semester and I was planning a study break for my residents. I went to a local store to buy some supplies—chips, drinks, that sort of thing. While I was there, I realized I forgot to get my little sister a Christmas present, so I got a "Hutter Hug Doll"—lots of other people at H.U. were getting them for their younger siblings. I also got a book that was on sale that I needed for a class the next semester. I went through the check-out line and paid for everything. As a state university, we are tax exempt, so I showed them the tax exempt card I got from my Resident Director, they took the tax off and I went back to the dorm to set up for the party. While I was setting up, I remembered that I had forgotten to separate the stuff I bought into two orders. No big deal, I thought, I'd just fill out the reimbursement form for the stuff for the party. A few days later while rushing off to one of my classes, I stopped by the Residence Life Office to fill out my reimbursement form. I filled it out for the whole amount of what I bought, turned it in, and went off to class. I didn't really even think about it. Right before I went home for break I got my reimbursement check. It came at a great time, as I had more shopping to do for the holidays, and I didn't get as much money from selling my textbooks at the end of the semester as I hoped or expected.

I came back for the spring semester and my RD said he needed to meet with me. He asked why there was a textbook and a doll on the receipt for the study break. I told him that I was sorry, but that in the rush of the end of the semester, I had forgotten to make it clear on the reimbursement form that I should only be reimbursed for the party stuff. Then he got this really concerned look on his face. He then asked if I realized that I used the tax exempt card for personal purchases. I told him I hadn't even thought about it. He then asked if I realized that in getting reimbursed for personal expenses that I'd taken state money. I hadn't really thought about that either. He explained that because I had misspent state funds, and not paid tax on personal expenses, that they had to let me go. I was fired.

Getting Some Advice

I was so angry that I went to the counseling center to talk with a therapist. She was really supportive. She also told me that misspending money is one of those things that can get you fired no matter where you work, or what kind of job you have—especially if it is government money. I learned that though I'm laid back, I need to be really careful about some things, and spending money is one of them.

A Second Chance

Though I did not get a second chance to be an RA, I've now graduated and have a full-time job. Getting fired was probably one of the best things that happened to me, because now I know to take spending really seriously. Better to be laid off as an RA than in a full-time job after graduation!

Lessons Learned

I never thought the biggest lesson I would learn as an RA would be the lesson that led to my not being an RA anymore. Like I said, I approach life in a laid back fashion—it is part of my charm. I would never do anything to intentionally hurt anyone. But, I ended up hurting myself when I didn't keep track of spending my money versus the university's money. I never thought it would be that big of a deal, but it is. If you can take one lesson away from this book, please don't do what I did. Be very careful about how you spend your programming budget. Don't ever spend it on a personal purchase. Be very careful about making this kind of mistake. I hope you learn from my experience. Have a great year!

Later,
Doug

Discussion Questions

1. What are the rules for spending money at your school?
2. What are the many reasons why it is important to follow them?
3. Do you think Doug's punishment was too harsh?
4. How will you make sure you don't make the same mistake?
5. What are the most helpful things you learned from this scenario?
6. How will you act differently as an RA, based on this new knowledge?

Tips for Spending Money

1. Always, always, always, follow the rules of your school exactly.
2. Even if you are the greatest RA in history, spending money the wrong way can get you fired.
3. Never spend school money for personal expenses.
4. Always keep receipts, or you can't get reimbursed.
5. Never overspend a budget.

30

Deciding what To Do Based on what Everyone Else Does

Dear Fellow RA,

Hi, my name is Ryon. I just finished my second year as an RA. I very nearly didn't have a second year as an RA because my transition to the job was pretty rocky. However, I made it through a tough transition, and have grown a lot from being on staff. I'm a student at "Laid Back University." We are pretty easy-going around here; nothing really fazes us much. We study some, party a good deal, and relax a lot. We're proud of our southern heritage and our chivalrous ways. It's a cool college experience.

The Situation

My first year in school I had a really laid back RA. He knew we'd drink on the hall and stuff. He didn't really care as long as we kept it out of his sight, or at least in a Solo cup. We smoked a little weed from time to time as well; as long as we burned incense at the same time, it wasn't a big deal. I really looked up to my RA—he was a great guy and I wanted to be like him. So, of course, I applied to be an RA for the next year and got the job.

I entered the year with only the perspective I had from my RA on how to do the job. During training, we had a lot of time to talk about our many different roles, policy enforcement, and all that stuff. I had a new RD in my building. He was from a really different school than ours. He was wrapped up pretty tight. Not a bad guy, but he had a lot to learn about how we do things at LBU. Each day of training during our staff meetings, he would talk about how to enforce policy, and he'd try to make us into little cops. We had one returning RA on our staff, Jason, who was really charismatic. He told us that what our RD said was a bunch of B.S. Jason told us that if we came across a party that was really getting out of hand, that instead of writing them up, we should just knock on the door, tell them to clear the room out, and let it all be over. I figured that made sense. So that is what I did.

I had my first few nights of duty and cleared out a few parties, but didn't turn in any incident reports or anything. No use in getting them in trouble, I figured. After fall break, I had a meeting with my RD, Jack. Jack asked me why he hadn't gotten any incident reports from me. I explained that I hadn't come across anything worth writing up. As we went on in our discussion, I ended up admitting that I hadn't been writing things up as he asked. He wasn't too happy about that.

Getting Some Advice

So Jack and I kept talking about my role, his perspectives, and mine. I realized that I had been hired to do a job, just as he had, and we both had a role to play. He explained to me all the reasons why it is important to document situations like parties. At first I resisted, but after awhile I saw what he meant. I told him that I had just done things the way I'd seen them done or others were doing too. He quickly helped me to see that "just because others do it that way" is a childish excuse, not an adult decision of taking responsibility. I felt kind of immature, but after I thought about it, I realized that doing what was uncomfortable for me was a way I could grow from my experience on staff, and in the end, was the right thing to do.

A Second Chance

The next weekend I was on duty, and I documented my first alcohol violation. It was kind of intimidating, and I felt a little odd because I had done the same kind of thing just the year before that I was writing up this group for; but I handled the situation without being too accusatory or getting in people's faces. Though they certainly weren't too happy about it, I was able to use a little humor to get them to do what I wanted. Moreover, I was acting with integrity—doing what I had agreed to do. That part of it wasn't easy, but did make me feel a little better about what I was doing. Sometimes adult decisions aren't easy.

Lessons Learned

Enforcing policy can be very difficult. As an RA, I learned that if you enjoy policy enforcement, there is probably something wrong with you. But if you don't do it, you aren't doing your job and your inaction could end up hurting someone. You may not think you should do things the way your RD tells you to at the beginning of the year, but it is his or her job to train you. You may be compelled to go along with a slack attitude you hear from a returning staff member, or you may excuse your lack of follow through by justifying it as the norm. In the end, though, the only thing you can fall back on is your integrity. Are you going to be the kind of person who keeps his or her word? Are you going to do what you've signed up to do? Or are you going to turn away from your responsibility? Being responsible isn't easy—it isn't meant to be. But it does help us grow, and makes us the adults we are becoming. I hope you learned from my experience.

Have a great year.

Bye,
Ryon

Discussion Questions

1. How do you go about deciding how to manage your role on staff with all the information and advice you get?
2. When is following the advice of others a good idea?
3. When is it not a good idea?
4. What are some ways to handle your frustration with a disagreement over your role that you have with your supervisor?
5. What are several reasons why it is important to enforce policy?

6. What could happen if we don't enforce policy?

7. Could you sympathize with Ryon in any way? If so, how?

8. What about the expectations that have been set for you; do you have a tough time accepting them?

9. Which of those expectations should you be talking about with your supervisor right now?

10. What are the most helpful things you learned from this scenario?

11. How will you act differently as an RA, based on this new knowledge?

Resources

Everybody Does It! Ethics & Everyday Choices
http://www.reslife.net/html/so-now_0802c.html
Emerging Leader—Resources for Effective Leadership
http://www.emergingleader.com/
Applied Ethics Resources on the Web
http://www.ethicsweb.ca/resources/
Student Leader Magazine
http://www.asgaonline.com/studentleader

Tips on Doing the Right Thing

1. "Johnny made me do it" only works in kindergarten.

2. If it is in your job description, or your supervisor says to do something in a certain way, doing so is the only honorable thing to do.

3. We show our integrity by aligning our actions with our words.

4. Not doing what we are expected to do can put others at risk.

5. When in doubt about an expectation, ask!

31

DATING A RESIDENT

Dear Fellow RA,

Hi! My name is Tamika. I attend Historically Black Central University (HBCU). We have a long tradition of educating talented African-American students from all over the United States. Most students major in either business administration or one of the social sciences. We have a lot of school pride (Go Bishops!), and a very strong alumni network. Last year I was an RA in a mixed dorm—we had first-year students and upper-class students, women and men. Our hall, Renardo Hall, was named after one of the founders of HBCU, Eliza Renardo.

So the year was OK. My women had a good time. Most of them were upper-class students and had their friends from before. I had a few first-year women on my floor, so I helped them get adjusted, learn about life at HBCU, and I helped them figure out how to manage their classes.

The Situation

At the beginning of the year, our House Director told us that we weren't supposed to date residents. I thought, whatever, that didn't apply to me. I had a guy I was dating back home and it wasn't something I needed to pay any attention to during training. By October, I broke up with Melvin from back home; I just wasn't dealing well with the long distance thing, and neither was he. It was mutual, so everything was alright.

During exams that fall, James, a resident from upstairs, asked if I wanted to go to a party at his friend's house to chill out. I figured what the heck. Looking back on it, I think James thought he was asking me out;

I just figured he was being friendly and we were both going to the same party. Anyway, we had a great time at the party and I ended up kissing him at the end of the night. It was nothing too out of hand (no tongue), just a friendly kiss. We both finished our exams, and that was about it.

When spring term started, so did we. I didn't think I liked him at first, but I started thinking about him over break and just couldn't get those cute dimples out of my mind. His eyes twinkle every time he smiles—that just kills me. So we started hanging out together all the time, and before long we were basically inseparable. I thought nothing of it in terms of my job. We were both mature adults. No big deal.

February came around and our campus had our annual Bishop Festival. It was a big weekend on campus where lots of alumni came back, there were always lots of parties, and everyone had a good time. Unfortunately, I got stuck being on duty for Saturday night, so I stayed in my room. When I walked around the hall for my 8 p.m. rounds, I heard a lot of noise and people's voices coming from James' room. They weren't spilling out into the hallway, and it was Bishop Festival weekend, so no big deal. When I walked back on that floor at 11 p.m., they were quiet, but there was another room on the floor where things were out of hand. I knocked on the door to tell them to keep it down, and James answered the door. I was pretty shocked because it wasn't his room. He had obviously been drinking, even though he's underage. He told me to just be cool and go away. I couldn't believe he put me in that position. I asked him to get the resident of the room for me. He told me that he knew I walked by his door earlier and did nothing about it, so obviously I could do the same thing now. I was so peeved that he put me in that position, and I felt a little bad about not doing anything about the noise in his room earlier that I wasn't sure what to say. I just left the room and went back to my room, not too sure what to do.

Getting Some Advice

I called my House Director and asked for advice on what to do. She suggested I go back to the room, ask to speak with the resident, determine if there was a policy violation, and if so, address it. I went back and did what I was supposed to do. Everyone made me out to be the hard-ass. It was unpleasant, to say the least. And the next day, James broke up with me. What a mess. I talked with my House Director about it. She was really helpful at putting everything into perspective for me. I hadn't really thought about how dating a resident might affect my role as an RA. My older brother always told me that I was the one in the family who had to learn things the hard way. I guess he was right. Lesson learned!

A Second Chance

This year I'm an RA again. I got asked out during the first week of school by a resident. This time, I declined, but we remained friends. It wasn't easy to say no, he had cute dimples too and was very athletic, but sometimes the easy thing to do and the right thing to do are two completely different things. Besides, there is always next year.

Lessons Learned

Things were much less tense for me in my second year as an RA. I really grew up a lot from the experience. You might not think that dating a resident is a big deal. You might think that it won't lead to problems. You might think that you are an adult and can make decisions for yourself. All of these might even be true, but, in the end, it is a lot easier if you decide not to date people when you are in a position of authority over them. It is more trouble than its worth, and can lead to a bunch of messes that you don't even want to deal with. I hope you learned from my experience. Have a great year!

Sincerely,
Tamika

Discussion Questions

1. What is your opinion of Tamika's decision to go with James to the party off campus?
2. What is your opinion of Tamika's decision to kiss James?

3. What are the many ways in which dating James affected Tamika in her role as an RA?

4. What are some different choices she could have made?

5. How did their dating potentially affect other residents?

6. Why is it important not to date a resident?

7. What is the policy of your school about dating residents?

8. What are the most helpful things you learned from this scenario?

9. How will you act differently as an RA, based on this new knowledge?

Resources

Sexual Harassment and Dating Residents
http://www.reslife.net/html/so-now_1201a.html
Question and Answer—Dating Your Resident
http://www.reslife.net/html/ask-ra_01.html

Tips on Dating Residents

1. Don't.

2. Dating people over whom we have power is inappropriate, and in many cases can be considered sexual harassment.

3. If you sense a relationship might develop, keep your distance.

4. If you aren't sure what to do, ask your supervisor.

5. There is always next year!

32

DRINKING ALCOHOL WITH UNDERAGE RESIDENTS

Dear Fellow RA,

My name is Ben. I attend Rural Country University, a small liberal arts college in the middle of nowhere Colorado. The scenery here is beautiful, but we have a pretty isolated campus. Not much to do in this town except what we can create for ourselves. Honestly, I can't believe I'm writing this letter to you. I never thought I'd be writing as a former RA. I had it all planned out—RA my sophomore year, do it again my junior year and show my leadership skills, and be a head resident my senior year. It didn't quite work out that way because of a decision I made toward the end of my sophomore year. Now that it is my senior year, I can look back on it with some perspective. At the time, it was tough.

The Situation

The guys on my floor were just great. Just about everyone got along well. Our hall was the place everyone in the building liked to hang out. We were socially active guys, always with a good story to share or random idea about what to do. I hung out on the floor with my guys a lot; they really looked up to me. That made me feel important—I didn't click with the guys on my hall last year, and to have a second chance at having friends on a first-year hall was like a fresh start for me. I made great friends with them. We hung out all the time. It was the best!

All year long my guys kept teasing me that at the end of the year, I'd have to get wasted with them. After all, they reasoned, at that point what did it matter? I'd joke back with them when they brought it up; inside I really did want to drink with them to just have one time where I didn't have that little thing in the back of my mind about being an authority figure. It was the one barrier between my residents and me. I wanted to knock it down like nobody's business.

Throughout the year, I got closer and closer to the edge. Sometimes I'd go off campus to a party and come home to the floor and act loopy—they all thought it was funny; no harm done. If my residents would go out to a party and come back a little bent, they'd often hang out in my room afterward to sober up. I had some really great conversations with them then—the kind you just don't have with guys when they are sober—you know what I mean?

As the year went on, the guys on the floor got a little more careless about hiding their alcohol. They would carry plastic cups into the hallway sometimes—I knew what was in there, but didn't know "for sure" so I let it slide. On Saturday mornings, the recycling container on our floor would have dozens of beer cans in it, but for all I knew some guys from off campus might have put them there, so I didn't say anything.

Well, as you might have guessed by now, the end of the year crept closer as the days went on. The guys on my floor planned a last day of classes party, and asked if I'd come. I told them that I'd really like to, but that I wanted to keep my job. They assured me that nobody would find out, and what did it matter anyway? It was the end of the year, our last chance to bond together as a floor and my only chance to drink with them. I said no, but inside I thought about it.

The last day of classes came; I was done by 2 p.m. I went from my last class to go hang out with some of my friends from last year and we had a few beers. Around 4 p.m. I went back to my room and my guys had obviously been drinking awhile. One of my best friends from the floor came into my room with two shot glasses. He gave me one, and he had the other. "To a great year," he said. I decided it was just one shot, and no one else was around, so why not? I took it, downed it, and told him to have a great time. After he left, a few minutes later I heard a lot of raucous laughter and, "No way!" "Seriously!?!" I soon figured that the one shot in my room was no longer a private matter. My residents then formed a parade, started singing a drinking song, and came into my room to get me. I couldn't resist, so I said what the hell and went with them. Suffice it to say that we had a great time that night and I got pretty loaded—as did they.

Getting Some Advice

The next day, my Area Director stopped by my room to ask why my floor was so messy. I explained that the guys on my floor had gotten a little out of hand the night before and that I'd take care of it. He then asked why someone had written on my door about how I was so cool and could drink with them anytime. I dodged the question, successfully I thought. Just then one of my residents came in my room and said "Man, you were so wasted last night, you were hysterical." He didn't know that the guy I was talking with was my AD. Oops. At that point, I had no choice but to admit what happened. Soon after, I was fired.

A Second Chance

While I didn't get a second chance to be an RA, I did get a chance to think about what is important to me. I got a chance to think about what the word "integrity" means. I had always thought of myself as an honest person who exceeds the expectations of his employer and always does a good job. My actions were not in line with that. I worked really hard in my summer jobs, and in other things I did on campus from then on to prove to myself that I could be a man of integrity. I feel a lot better about myself now.

Lessons Learned

Getting fired was a tough pill for me to swallow. At first, I thought my AD was being a jackass. In thinking about it later though, I understood that I had gone against what I promised to do when I accepted my job as an RA. As much as I wanted to be friends with my residents, I got so close to them that I wasn't able to fulfill my responsibilities. One of the guys on my floor actually developed a pretty bad drinking problem that year, and I didn't notice because I wasn't doing my job.

I felt bad about that. I also felt bad when I had to tell my parents that I wouldn't have free housing by being an RA the next year. That was tough. They made me get a second job over the summer to make up for the difference. My summers were no fun because of that—I just had to work all the time. One night of fun was really not worth it. I hope you learn from my experience. Have a great year!

Be good,

Ben

Discussion Questions

1. What were several decision points Ben had throughout the year about addressing alcohol?
2. What were several decision points Ben had throughout the last day of classes?
3. What were the decisions Ben could have made differently?
4. What decisions do you think Ben should have made differently?
5. Would any of those decisions have been different if Ben was of legal drinking age versus being underage?
6. Can you sympathize with any of the decisions Ben made?
7. What consequences did Ben's decisions have for himself? His residents?
8. Why is it important not to violate policy with your residents?
9. What are the most helpful things you learned from this scenario?
10. How will you act differently as an RA, based on this new knowledge?

Resources

You Hold the Key: The RA/Friend Relationship
http://www.reslife.net/html/so-now_1002a.html
The Ultimate Ethical Dilemma of an RA: Friendship or Policy?
http://www.reslife.net/html/so-now_0203a.html
Thoughts on Behavior and the RA Job: It's a lot About Role Modeling

http://www.reslife.net/html/so-now_0102b.html
Underage Drinking Enforcement Training Center
http://www.udetc.org/
Secondary Effects of Heavy Drinking on Campus
http://www.edc.org/hec/pubs/factsheets/secondary-effects.html

Tips on Alcohol and Residents

1. They don't mix.
2. If you have residents who drink, they will probably ask you to join them. Decide right now how you will say no, so doing so becomes your natural response.
3. If you find that you are tempted to break this rule, get out of the building and go somewhere else.
4. If the feeling persists, talk with your supervisor about what to do.
5. Be sure that your residents are following policy and the law at all times.

33

STAFF CONFLICT

Dealing with a Slacking Staff Member

Dear Fellow RA,

My name is Julia. I grew up in a suburb outside Detroit and I attend a small private college in Ohio, Shonka College. Here at SC we have great residence halls; about 90% of students live on campus. Being an RA is one of the most competitive and respected things to do. We get about five applications for every open RA spot. That's why I was so thrilled last year when I was offered an RA position. I just knew it would be great, that my fellow staff members would be totally awesome, and that it would be a great way to spend my senior year.

I was mostly right. It's now the end of my first year as an RA, and it has been mostly great. The women on my hall got along well; even though they already had lots of friends coming into the year, they still came out for my programs and hung out together from time to time. The "mostly" part wouldn't be necessary except there was one thing this year that has been a royal pain, or I guess I should say one person, Scott. Scott is a nice guy and everything, don't get me wrong, but he has been a really big pain to work with on a day to day basis. I guess I should admit up front that I am a very organized person; I pride myself on doing my job well, showing up on time to meetings, getting things done correctly, that sort of thing. Scott is, well, not like me. He's so laid back that he's practically comatose. Sometimes I think he doesn't do his job just to annoy me.

The Situation

It all started on opening day. Scott showed up five minutes before check-in and hadn't set up his portion of the table yet. As a staff we all agreed to decorate our table with welcome signs and Shonka College memorabilia. Scott showed up with an "SC" plastic cup (the kind they use at frat parties for beer), set it on our table and said "that's my contribution," sat down at the table and put his feet up (his *bare* feet). I was furious! I had worked all night making cut-out-flowers for our welcome signs and was greeting people in the parking lot as they got ready to check in. Scott was just sleeping his butt off and not doing anything to help that whole time. What a jerk! I didn't say anything to him though, in the name of "staff bonding" and unity. I let it slide.

When it was Scott's turn for duty, he never showed up in the duty office on time. My room was closest to the office, so when he was on duty, I'd know it because everyone came to my room for help. They all started out with the same thing "There's no one in the duty office so...." I covered for him, thinking things would get better. As you guessed by now, they didn't. His residents were always making noise and disturbing the women on my floor. Then one day I saw him leaving the building for a fall semi-formal on the same night he was scheduled to have duty. I just lost it. I screamed at him in front of a whole bunch of people about how he had duty, how I wasn't going to cover for him anymore, and how he was just basically a waste of oxygen on the face of the earth. He just stared at me, called me a name I will not repeat here, and went on his way. It turns out, he had already switched duty with someone else, I just didn't ask about it.

Getting Some Advice

After making a fool out of myself, I called my friend from high school, Michelle. Michelle was an RA at her school too and was a great listener. I told her all about what happened all year, and tonight, and she listened intently. Then she asked if talked with him the day after opening about how I felt. I said no. She asked if I talked with him about being late for duty to tell him how it affected me. Again, I said no. You can see where this conversation was heading. I didn't give Scott the benefit of a conversation. He didn't know how much I resented him, nor did he know why. Now of course, a lot of the stuff he did was not excusable under any circumstances. But still, I owed him feedback, which I denied to him out of my own desire to avoid conflict.

A Second Chance

I thought a lot about Michelle's advice over the winter break, and realized I needed to have a talk with Scott—one that was long overdue. When we got back to school in January, I asked him if we could get together to talk about last semester. He said sure. When we did, I was surprised at how calm he was about the whole thing. Once I talked with him and explained where I was coming from, he really heard me. I asked him to tell me more about his working style and why he did things like he did. We both learned a lot about each other, and how to get along better. We will never approach our job the same way, but we've learned how best to work with each other. I should have had that conversation with him a long time ago; it sure would have helped both of us.

Lessons Learned

The thing I learned most from being an RA is really twofold. First, always ask a question before jumping to conclusions. Second, talk through your conflicts instead of avoiding them. Avoidance can result in a later explosion, and that just isn't a good idea for anyone. So if you have that one staff member who drives you nuts, sit down and talk with him. Find out what makes him tick. Give him the benefit of understanding where you come from. Then hopefully, you both will get along much better and have a great year. I hope you learned from my situation. Have a great year!

Most sincerely,

Julia

Discussion Questions

1. Under what circumstances should we discuss our frustrations with fellow staff members with them?
2. What approaches to such discussions are possible, and what are some likely outcomes?
3. At what point do we discuss the issue with a supervisor?
4. Why should we have these discussions?
5. Why might we avoid having these discussions?
6. What are the most helpful things you learned from this scenario?
7. How will you act differently as an RA, based on this new knowledge?

Resources

Developing a Strong Staff Team
http://www.reslife.net/html/tools_0701b.html
The Conflict Resolution Information Source
http://www.crinfo.org/

Tips on Dealing with Slackers

1. Don't take their lack of performance personally—they probably aren't slacking to annoy you.
2. Start by giving them the benefit of the doubt—there may be something going on in their life that you don't know about.
3. Talk it out.
4. Avoid confronting the person; focus on discussing the behavior and how you perceive it.
5. Focus on listening to their side before jumping to conclusions.

34

Dealing with Parents

Dear Fellow RA,

Hi. My name is Liz. I attend Schonour University, a small public university located in a small rural town in Oregon. I'm a psychology major and I plan to go to graduate school in order to become a psychotherapist. This is my first year as an RA. In addition to being involved on campus, I also attend a local church in town and volunteer at the local battered women's shelter. As I write this, it is spring break (I have duty, so there is not much else to do right now).

The Situation

A few weeks ago I was at the local grocery store, and I ran into the mother of one of the women who lives on my floor. I know the family well—they go to the same church where I have gone every Sunday for three years and I've been over to their house for dinner a few times. I was so thrilled when Sally, their daughter, was assigned to my floor as a resident. One day I ran into Sally's mom at the grocery store. We were in the produce section and she asked me if she could speak with me confidentially about Sally, who she suspected was a lesbian. She said it all so quickly I didn't know how to react. I know that Sally is a lesbian. Sally's mom said she was very concerned about her health and safety, and just wanted to be helpful to her daughter. I made a joke out of the situation and walked away to the cereal aisle. I wasn't really sure how to handle it.

Getting Some Advice

After getting back from the store, I wasn't really sure what to do. Sally's mom is not someone I can avoid—I see her every week. I didn't know how I should respond when she inevitably brought up the issue again. So, I decided to talk with the Dean of Students (who was also around during Spring Break). The Dean and I talked about it for a long time. After talking it through, we decided that if Sally's mom ever asked me that or another personal question about Sally then I would simply say "that's something you would need to ask Sally about, right?" We also decided that because my primary relationship and responsibility was to my resident, that I should tell Sally about her mom's question. This was not an easy decision to make, as the simplest thing to do would be to just ignore the fact that I ever had that conversation with her mom. But I decided that if it were my mom asking my RA about something personal, I'd want to know about it. So after Spring Break was over, I told Sally about running into her mom. She was taken aback at first, but was really glad that I told her.

A Second Try

Sure enough, a week later I saw Sally's mom, and she asked the same question. I quickly responded that she should ask Sally about that and not me. Her mom was actually a little embarrassed. I thought I'd be the uncomfortable one, but when I put things back in her court, she saw that she shouldn't have put me in that position.

Lessons Learned

The biggest lesson I learned as an RA is that our first responsibility is to our residents, not to their families, friends, or others. Though we don't have doctor/patient confidentiality, we do have private relationships with our residents and should not divulge their personal information to others except to our supervisor when required to do so. I learned that when it comes to my residents, that protecting their confidentiality is a critical factor in keeping their trust. I hope you learn from my situation. Have a great year!

Yours truly,
Liz

Discussion Questions

1. What are the different major issues with which this scenario deals?
2. What are the available choices Liz had at different parts of the story?
3. What are the advantages and disadvantages of those options?
4. Do you agree with her decision in the grocery store?
5. Do you agree with her decision to tell Sally about the interaction with her mom?
6. Do you agree with the way Liz dealt with Sally's mom the second time?
7. What are the most helpful things you learned from this scenario?
8. How will you act differently as an RA, based on this new knowledge?

Resources

U.S. Department of Education—FERPA
http://www.ed.gov/policy/gen/guid/fpco/ferpa/index.html

Tips on Dealing with Inquisitive Parents

1. It is against the law (FERPA) for you to share certain types of personal information about your residents with anyone (even their parents) without their permission.
2. Your primary relationship is with your residents. Keep it that way!

3. Even if you think you are doing a good thing, you should not be sharing a resident's private matters with others (except of course your supervisor when expected).

4. Be friendly but firm with nosey parents.

5. Keep the trust of your residents; tell them if an unauthorized person asks for their personal information.

PART 7

SAFETY AND SECURITY

CHAPTER 35 NOT GETTING EVERYONE OUT DURING A FIRE
         ALARM

CHAPTER 36 TRYING TO HELP A RAPE SURVIVOR BUT
         MAKING HER FEEL WORSE

CHAPTER 37 DEALING WITH SOMEONE WHO IS NOT A STUDENT

CHAPTER 38 EXCUSING VIOLENT BEHAVIOR AS "JUST
         BLOWING OFF STEAM"

Keeping watch over the safety and security of our residents is one of the main bits of bedrock for the RA position. After all, if our residents aren't safe, how can they possibly make friends, learn, and live in community? J.T.'s style is fairly laid back in chapter 35. He learns, though, how important it is to get everyone out of the building during fire alarm. In chapter 36, Emily means well, but ends up completely mishandling a situation where she should support a resident who was raped. Next, in chapter 37, Amy has a curve ball thrown at her she never expected and doesn't handle it very well; but learning from her experience can certainly help you do better. Finally, in chapter 38, we all learn to stop violence before it starts escalating like it did with Joe's residents.

35

NOT GETTING EVERYONE OUT DURING A FIRE ALARM

Dear Fellow RA,

Hi. My name is J.T. I go to a small to midsized public university in the Southeast, "Colonial University." Here at CU we have a very strong sense of community; most people live in residence halls. Many students stay close friends with their freshman hallmates all four years and beyond. We are an academically challenging institution. We are not really a party school, but if you want to do just about anything you can find it somewhere.

The Situation

My leadership style is serious but laid back. I get my work done, and do what I need to do to take care of the guys on my hall. I'm one who believes that you should take care of the big stuff (keep them from getting too out of hand, make sure they have a good year, etc.) and let the details work themselves out. At the beginning of the year the fire alarm system in our building was having trouble, so it kept going off about three times a week. It wasn't that big a deal when it was 3 p.m. on Saturday afternoon, but 5 a.m. on a Tuesday morning was a real drag. Most of my residents usually got out, except a few who were hard sleepers or who had "visitors" with them. During the first scheduled fire alarm, only about half of my residents came out. My Area Director got all up in my face about it, so I said I'd take care of it in the future. I told my guys at our next meeting that they'd need to get out when the alarm went off so I could keep the AD off my back. For the most part, they listened.

Then in November, one of my residents, Joe, was microwaving a burrito and he hit 20 minutes instead of two minutes—and he left his room. Of course, it was at four in the morning, and, of course, the fire alarm went off. I got up and yelled down the hallway to get out and then I went outside with my blanket wrapped around me and sat there all annoyed. My degree of annoyance though was nothing compared to my AD's. About 10 minutes after the alarm went off, half of my residents left the building one-by-one, followed by my AD. My AD came up to me and asked why I didn't follow protocol and make sure they left the building. I told him it was just a burrito and there was no sense getting all uptight about it. That didn't go over too well. Long story short, I ended up on probation as a staff member and just didn't understand what the big deal was.

Getting Some Advice through a New Experience

A couple days later, the residence hall across the street from us, Helvey Hall, caught on fire. This was not just a little fire, but the kind where the flames were shooting 25 feet above the roof and every fire truck within 30 miles came. It happened at about noon, so everyone was awake or in class. When it went off, the RAs were in class, but fortunately there was a maintenance worker in the building who went through the building to get everyone out. The building really burned fast—had the worker not gotten everyone out so quickly, someone would have surely died. It is quite an experience to watch a building burn—especially one you look at every day and know the people who live there. As I looked at the building burning down, I realized why it is so important that we get every resident out of our buildings when the fire alarm goes off. The point my AD was trying to make to me before got through when I watched Helvey burn to the ground.

A Second Chance

Now whenever a fire alarm goes off, I make sure all of my residents leave, period. No excuses. I'm not going to have someone I care about die in a fire. That's really what can happen if people like you and me don't make sure everyone leaves. Residents might think we are overreacting; they might think we're being a tight wad, they might complain. Let them complain. I'd rather have a complaining resident than a dead one.

Lessons Learned

I will never again take a fire alarm as an inconvenience. Sure, it could be inconvenient to get out of bed at 4 a.m. for a burned burrito, but it is worth it for that one time when it might be many lives at stake. As an RA I learned that we need to set the standard of behavior for our residents. If we take something seriously, they are much more likely to do so as well. If we don't take something seriously, they surely won't. I hope you learned from my experience. Have a great year.

Peace,

J. T.

Discussion Questions

1. Why is it tempting to be laid back during fire alarms?
2. Do you sympathize with J.T.'s earlier perspective? Why?
3. Do you think probation was appropriate for J.T.? Why or why not?
4. What are some effective ways of getting residents to learn to get out during a fire?
5. What are the protocols on your campus for getting people out during a fire?
6. How do these differ from the approach J.T. took?
7. What are the most helpful things you learned from this scenario?
8. How will you act differently as an RA, based on this new knowledge?

Resources

The Center for Campus Fire Safety
http://www.campusfire.org/index.html
U.S. Fire Administration—College Fire Safety
http://www.usfa.fema.gov/safety/atrisk/campus/
Campus Firewatch
http://www.campus-firewatch.com/
National Fire Prevention Association
http://www.nfpa.org/index.asp

Tips on Fire Alarms

1. Get everyone out, right away, every time!
2. Staying inside a building while an alarm is going off is illegal.
3. Staying inside during a fire alarm can lead to death.
4. It's not hard to evacuate; just leave!
5. Take every single alarm seriously; get people out quickly and in an orderly fashion.

36

TRYING TO HELP A RAPE SURVIVOR BUT MAKING HER FEEL WORSE

Dear Fellow RA,

Hi! My name is Emily. I'm an RA at a small private liberal arts college in the Midwest, Haygood University. About 50% of students at HU live on campus. This is my second year as an RA. Last year, I made my biggest mistake by trying to help one of my residents who was sexually assaulted; I ended up doing everything wrong (at least in the beginning). Here is what happened.

The Situation

Sarah was a woman on my hall who liked to go out a lot to parties. She frequently stayed out late and often came home drunk along with a clique of her friends who lived on the hall near her room. One night in the spring she went out with Stephen, a guy she'd been seeing off and on all year. He was a nice guy who lived upstairs from us. Everybody liked him; he was on the soccer team and was a member of a popular fraternity. The next morning I walked by Sarah's door and heard her crying. I knocked on the door and she didn't answer. After a few knocks I discovered the door was unlocked, so I went in and asked Sarah why she was crying. She was just sitting on her bed in a daze, alternating between crying and staring off into space. She kept saying "It's all my fault" over and over again. I asked her what was her fault, and she didn't respond at all—it was like I wasn't even there. Then finally, I demanded to know what her problem was. Sarah told me that she and Stephen were doing shots in his room and then they went off to a party at a house off campus. There he gave her three beers and five cups of "Electric Lemonade" —a kind of punch that had some combination of tequila, vodka, and gin in it. Sarah said that she started feeling sick, so Stephen took her back to his room. After Sarah threw up in a trash can, she started to pass out on Stephen's bed. She's not sure how much time passed, but she woke up with his penis inside of her, thrusting back and forth. Sarah said she was so drunk that when she tried to push him off, she didn't have the strength to do anything, and was so surprised and confused about what was happening that she couldn't even say a word. After it was over, she threw up again, came down the stairs, and passed out again in her bed. Now she had just remembered bits and pieces of what happened that night. Sarah insisted that it was all her fault for getting drunk and going back to his room with him.

The first thing I said to her after she relayed the story was that it was good that she was taking responsibility for her behavior. I told her that Stephen seemed like such a nice guy, and asked if she was sure that she didn't lead him on and consent to having intercourse; after all, why did she go back to his room with him to begin with? I also told her that she shouldn't have been drinking so much, and perhaps this incident would teach her that she should be more careful about how much she drinks when she goes out. I reiterated that doing shots is dangerous; even more dangerous is drinking punch when you don't know how much alcohol is in it. I then told Sarah to be sure she told her roommate what happened, because she had the right to know why she was so upset. I also told her to be sure to call her parents to tell them what happened, and that I'd come talk with her again tomorrow to fill out an incident report.

I really thought I was doing all the right things, but everything I said to her made her seem more and more detached from what I was saying. I decided to go to the Sexual Assault Response Coordinator on campus to ask for some advice.

Getting Some Advice

Wow. I don't think there was much more I could have done that was hurtful or just plain wrong. After talking with Dr. Jackson, I learned that I did just about everything as poorly as possible. First off, I began by barging my way into her room and demanding that she tell me what happened. While this was effective at getting information from her, one of the only bits of control she had left was over who knew about what happened, and I forced it out of her. That was the last kind of disposition she needed to have in someone around her. I learned that when I praised her for taking responsibility for her behavior and asked if she led him on, why she went to his room, if she was sure she didn't consent, and that she shouldn't have been drinking so much, it just made things a lot worse. Dr. Jackson told me that many rape survivors blame themselves for what happened, even though it was the man's decision to rape them. In this case, Sarah made some judgments that increased her risk of being vulnerable; however, she did not make the decision for Stephen to rape her; for that, he was responsible. Given her level of intoxication, she was incapable of giving consent. A lecture on drinking is the last thing she needed to hear at this moment; rather, she needed some reassurance that it was Stephen's choice, indeed his fault, that the rape occurred. I blew it further by insisting there were other people she needed to tell (these things should be her choice) and by saying I'd need to talk with her about it again to fill out an incident report. Of course, at my school we are required to tell our supervisors if a rape occurs, however, the way I told this to Sarah was curt and insensitive.

After pointing out the multiple ways I made things worse, Dr. Jackson gave me some advice on what might be helpful to Sarah. First, she told me that no two survivors are the same, and that any advice she would give me would apply to most, but not all survivors and most, but not all of the time. She noted that the most important thing was to encourage Sarah to get immediate medical attention. She explained that it is important that the survivor go to the hospital for medical attention, particularly in the first three days after the assault. This will also allow her to save evidence, so she can decide later whether to be a witness in a criminal or university case against Stephen. This medical attention will include STI testing, pregnancy counseling, and treatment of her injuries. Dr. Jackson explained that survivors may even have internal injuries of which they are not aware. Given that I had been so forceful with Sarah before, Dr. Jackson reminded me that all I could really do is suggest that she go to the hospital and take her if she wants to go. If she doesn't want to go right away, I needed to remember that it's her choice not to go. My next task was to address whether or not Sarah felt safe living in her room, particularly with Stephen living upstairs. I needed to explain the various options to her about relocating according to the policies here at RU. Next, Dr. Jackson suggested that I focus more on listening to her rather than either suggesting why it happened, asking lots of questions, or judging her statements. Instead, she suggested I remember this simple rule: it's better to talk less and listen more.

Given that the single most important factor in a woman's recovery from rape is whether or not she is believed, Dr. Jackson stressed that I should believe what Sarah was telling me, paying careful attention not to blame her or agree if she blames herself. Even though I think Sarah made some bad decisions with regard to alcohol, I needed to remember that no one ever deserves to be raped. Dr. Jackson cautioned me that it was likely that Sarah would take a long time to make simple decisions. She encouraged me to wait patiently while she decided small things; making small decisions now will help give her the confidence to make bigger decisions later. Finally, and perhaps obviously, she recommended that I tell Sarah about all of the on and off campus resources available, and offer to come with her to see Dr. Jackson or another counselor to talk about what happened.

A Second Chance

Later that day I went to see Sarah again. I can't say it was a great conversation, but by following Dr. Jackson's advice, it went a lot better than my first conversation with her, and it was a lot more helpful. Although I can't undo the damage that Stephen did to her, nor can I undo the damage I did to her by blaming her for it and lecturing her about it, I was set on a course to be much more helpful than before.

Lessons Learned

I learned that surviving a sexual assault is much more complicated than I ever imagined. I also learned that some of my instincts on how to interact with a survivor were way off base. I guess I realized how much more I needed to learn about how to be supportive with a sexual assault survivor. My greatest hope is that you will learn more about sexual assault before it happens to one of your residents. In the year 2000, a study by the U.S. Department of Justice found that roughly one in four college women have survived either rape or attempted rape in their lifetime. The study also found that 3% of college women survive rape or attempted rape every school year. So, if you have 30 women on your floor, odds are that 7 or 8 have experienced rape or attempted rape before, and one will this year. Please learn as much as you can about it, so you can help your resident far better than I helped Sarah. I hope you learned from my experience. Have a great year.

Love ya!
Emily

Discussion Questions

1. Why might Emily have reacted the way she did initially with Sarah?
2. What is the difference between using bad judgment and being responsible for what happens in a bad situation?
3. What are some of the things Emily did that made Sarah worse off?
4. What are some of the things that we should do to help survivors recover?
5. What are the policies and procedures here at our school that we should know about regarding sexual assault?
6. What are the resources available here at our school that we should know about regarding sexual assault?
7. What are the most helpful things you learned from this scenario?
8. How will you act differently as an RA, based on this new knowledge?

Resources

The Rape, Abuse, and Incest National Network
http://www.rainn.org
One in Four
http://www.nomorerape.org
The National Sexual Violence Resource Center
http://www.nsvrc.org/
The U.S. Office for Victims of Crime
http://www.ojp.usdoj.gov/ovc/
The White Ribbon Campaign
http://www.whiteribbon.ca/get_involved/default.asp?load=org-kit
The National Sex Offender Public Registry
http://www.nsopr.gov/
The National Center for Victims of Crime
http://www.ncvc.org/ncvc/main.aspx?dbID=dash_Home

Tips on Helping Rape Survivors

1. Show the survivor nonverbally and verbally that you believe what she (or he) is telling you.
2. Talk less, listen more.
3. Get the survivor to the hospital immediately if she or he is willing to go.
4. Be patient with the survivor's decisions; they will take a long time to make.
5. Refer the survivor to counseling; offer to go along the first time if it helps.

37

DEALING WITH SOMEONE WHO IS NOT A STUDENT

Dear Fellow RA,

Hey! My name is Amy. I've been an RA for two years at Canterbury College in rural Pennsylvania. CC is a small school with a very strong campus community. We live in a safe, rural area and we've never had a problem with off-campus people causing trouble in our residence halls. When I was in my first year as an RA, my residents often had friends or boyfriends from home or another school come to visit. They would sometimes stay a few days and it was never a big deal. I never reminded my residents of school policy or attempted to enforce the rule that visitors cannot stay more than 48 hours and should be escorted at all times. I never even really bothered to keep track of who had visitors or who the visitors were. I had my own bathroom and never really ran into visitors in the hall bathroom. This hands-off treatment of hall visitors ended up being damaging to my floor.

The Situation

One of my residents, Cathryn, was friendly and outgoing and was someone who seemed pretty independent. I would often say hi to her, but had never really gotten to know her well. One Tuesday afternoon, I was returning from lunch at the dining hall with friends when I noticed an ambulance and police cars pulled up right next to my residence hall, lights flashing and all. Needless to say, I was freaked out and ran in to see what was going on. The police were gathered on my floor and were packed in around Cathryn's room. As I got closer I noticed there was blood on the hallway floor and I heard crying from inside her room. I was becoming more and more alarmed as I got closer. Inside was Cathryn and her roommate, Diane, both were bawling and trying to tell the campus police officer what had happened.

Apparently, Cathryn's boyfriend, Nathan, had come to visit her and had been staying in her room for about a week. While Cathryn was in class, Nathan stayed in her room and watched TV. That day, he decided to sign onto Instant Messenger with Cathryn's screen-name and started IM'ing people pretending to be Cathryn. One of the people he IM'ed was Cathryn's male friend from home. Nathan started typing things like "I've always liked you" and other suggestive stuff in an attempt to get a reaction from the guy he was IM'ing. The guy from back home thought Cathryn was joking and started to joke back, "Is that why you're always trying to make-out with me?" Nathan, in a jealous fit, didn't take it as a joke. When Cathryn returned from class with Diane, Nathan began to scream and curse at Cathryn, calling her horrible names and saying really mean stuff. He was so enraged and so out of control that he picked up a pair of scissors from Cathryn's desk and stabbed himself in the neck with them. The residents next door were alert enough to call Campus Police almost immediately. The police arrived quickly and got the boyfriend to an ambulance.

I was extremely upset at the whole incident and the women on my floor were definitely freaked out by the situation. Once the police left, I was so upset I didn't know what to do. I just wanted to be sure that that type of situation would never happen again, so I went to the Dean's office and demanded that Cathryn be moved out of the hall. In my mind it was her fault for having this visitor who was obviously mentally unstable on my floor. By blaming the whole situation on Cathryn, I thought it would fix things for my residents. A few days of confusion went by while the Dean's office tried to sort things out, make sure the boyfriend was recovering, and clean up the blood. Meanwhile the women on my hall had totally ostracized Cathryn and, like me, blamed her for what had happened.

Getting Some Advice

The Dean of Students invited me to talk with her about the whole situation. She let me vent about how upset I was about the situation, and how all my residents were in an uproar. We then talked about how my residents were likely to take a cue from me as to how to react to the incident. By freaking out, I was basically giving them license to get all upset as well, which wasn't helping anyone. Also, by blaming the situation on Cathryn, I was hurting a resident, and giving implicit permission to other residents to be hurtful to Cathryn as well—during a time when she really needed our support. The Dean had also talked with Diane, and heard that she was bothered about having a guy in her room for a week, but because I hadn't said anything about visitors being a possible problem, she didn't want to cause problems and seem stuffy by coming to me about it. My casual attitude had led Cathryn, and all of my residents, to believe that it was perfectly acceptable to have her boyfriend basically living with her for a week and being in the hall when she wasn't there. By not trying to stay on top of who was visiting and how long they were staying, I had totally blinded myself to any possible problems with visitors. After I realized everything I had done wrong, I felt rather foolish.

A Second Chance

I had really blown it with Cathryn, and honestly, we didn't get along too well for the rest of the year. She ended up moving to a different building, as she was so embarrassed about the whole situation. For me, in this situation, getting a second chance didn't happen so much with Cathryn, as it did with me keeping a better eye on who was visiting our hall, for how long, and how it was affecting everyone involved. I didn't take on the role of a police officer, but I did keep track of who was around, and made sure that my residents did all they could to make everyone else comfortable and safe.

Lessons Learned

I learned too many lessons to count from this situation. I certainly learned not to overreact to a situation on my floor. I certainly learned not to blame a resident and ostracize her for what her friends do. Of course, residents are responsible for their guest's behavior, but the solution is not to lead a revolt against the resident. I learned to be more careful about enforcing the guest policy for my building, and why that policy was important. I also learned to calm down before making any decisions about how to proceed when a situation seems out of control. I hope you learned from my experience. Have a great year!

Truly yours,
Amy

Discussion Questions

1. What kind things could Amy have done/said to let her residents know about school policy on visitors?
2. Why is it important to set standards on your floor and not leave things open to interpretation?
3. What are some ways in which Amy could have handled the situation before it happened? After it happened?
4. Why is it important to not blame Cathryn for what happened?
5. What are some strategies you could use to keep tabs on who is visiting without seeming nosey or intrusive?
6. What are the most helpful things you learned from this scenario?
7. How will you act differently as an RA, based on this new knowledge?

Resources

Security on Campus, Inc.
http://www.securityoncampus.org/
Critical Incidents—Response and Reaction

http://www.residentassistant.com/advice/criticalincidents.htm
Campus Safety Health and Environmental Management Association
http://www.cshema.org
Office of Post-Secondary Education—Campus Security Statistics
http://www.ope.ed.gov/security/

Tips on Nonstudents and Trauma on the Floor

1. Nonstudents are unlikely to respect your authority. Talk to the resident they are visiting to get through to the nonstudent.
2. If a serious incident occurs, stay calm.
3. Be careful not to blame your resident for a guest's outlandish behavior. The resident is ultimately responsible of course, but may have had no idea what would happen.
4. Always use your support system of fellow staff and your supervisor when things get tough.
5. Take things one step at a time!

38

EXCUSING VIOLENT BEHAVIOR AS "JUST BLOWING OFF STEAM"

Dear Fellow RA,

My name is Joe and I'm from the Midwestern plain states. I've been an RA at "Windy University" for three years now. WU is a state school where most everyone who applies is accepted. Most of our students come here from within the state. Although it isn't that hard to get admitted, it is highly thought of in the state to go here. Almost every family in the state who has a college graduate in the house has a family member who went here. There are basically only two schools people go to in this state: here, and Tech. It has been said that if a WU alum marries an alumni from Tech it is a "mixed marriage." Football is our state's main pastime; and we aren't shy about getting a little physical on the field. About a third of our students live on campus in the residence halls. The rest live in the fraternities and sororities and in nearby houses and apartments. My first year on staff was definitely the toughest. My residents were cool and all, but they tended to take things a little too seriously and were a little over the top.

The Situation

The "situation" on my hall was more of a series of situations that led to things getting out of control. In early September, my hall formed an intramural rugby team. Our first game was with a rival residence hall. Everyone on my floor was trying to prove himself as being tough. So, when the other team would get more physical, my guys would pound back twice as hard. At the end of the first game we just barely lost. A few of my residents had an exchange of words with the captain of the other team and a fight broke out. It wasn't that serious, but a few guys on each team needed a stitch or two. I basically just figured that they were all just blowing off steam so it was no big deal.

On a couple weekends during the semester, I noticed that some of my residents would come back in from parties looking like they'd been in a scuffle. Usually they didn't end up going to the hospital or anything, so it wasn't too serious. Guys around here just settle their differences by pounding on each other every once in awhile. My residents were physical guys, and that is just what happens sometimes.

There was this really obnoxious kid who lived upstairs, Billy. He looked like a good stiff wind could knock him over. He was all of five feet four inches tall. If he was more than a buck twenty I'd be surprised. He was kind of like a little gnat that just wouldn't go away. One day I heard his RA say in a staff meeting that he was worried about Billy. It seems that Billy had a plan to find someone with really rich parents, pick a fight with him, lose, and sue the heck out of him for as much money as possible. Now that is sick. I thought "what a loser" but didn't give it much more thought.

About a week later, Billy was walking around my floor making an idiot of himself, as he often does to attract whatever attention he can. It looked like he'd been drinking a fair bit, but he wasn't too drunk. As he passed by one of my residents, Billy nudged him in the shoulder and just kept going. My resident just blew it off, as did I. What a little twerp. Well, Billy kept coming back up and down the hall. He started singing stupid songs, replacing words in them to insult different guys on my floor. One of my bigger residents, Joe, yelled from inside his room "Hey Billy, get your candy ass out of our hall or I'll squish you like the little gnat that you are." I heard the comment from my room, but I had heard worse before. It sounded like just the usual banter. Later on I went out for the evening with some friends.

When I got back, I heard that about 15 minutes after I left, Billy came back to the hall with a squirt gun filled with perfume and sprayed it all over Joe's neck, face, and shoulders. That was enough for Joe, as he popped him one good in the jaw. Unfortunately, Joe hit Billy hard enough that his jaw broke, and he had to go to the hospital for surgery to have it fused back together. Billy ended up with his lawsuit. After a long, drawn out series of judicial proceedings, appeals, attempts to influence the process by powerful people fighting on both sides of the fence, Joe ended up expelled and Billy got his $500 thousand.

Getting Some Advice

In retrospect, I felt like an idiot. I should have seen this all coming. I went and talked with a professor I took for a seminar about violence. We talked about some of the reasons why men engage in violence, how gender roles fit in, and how masculinity is involved. We talked about the different chances I had to set a nonviolent example but didn't make the most of it. We also talked about how I had the chance to intervene as a bystander when I saw either a violent incident or an incident that could become violent and did nothing. I vowed to never stand by again and do nothing when a situation might get out of hand.

A Second Chance

The next year when one of my residents started fronting with another resident, I calmly talked with both of them and got them to see how ridiculous they were being. The other guys on my floor got the message quickly, and we had a great year. Sure, it wasn't a perfect year and I'm not saying they were angels, but we made violence a bad word on my floor. It wasn't an option if you wanted respect. And that made all the difference.

Lessons Learned

Going through the experience with Billy on my floor taught me a lot. Sometimes kids who pick fights have bigger issues they are dealing with and they need help. Sometimes guys turn to violence as their first option because they don't yet have the tools to resolve conflict in other ways. It is important for those of us who are on staff to learn how to reach out to troubled students, to model nonviolence, and to never tolerate it in our midst. Violence is never the answer. I wish I had learned that lesson before, but I surely know it now. I hope you are able to take something away from my experience. Have a great year.

Hang in there,

Joe

Discussion Questions

1. Identify the multiple times when Joe could have stepped in to say something about his resident's violent behavior.
2. What could Joe have said or done in each circumstance? What are some possible responses?
3. How can we work together to make violence unacceptable?
4. Why might some people, particularly men, choose violence as a behavior?
5. What are some ways we can address this on a personal level?
6. Why is it important to end violence?
7. What kind of difference can one person make who seeks to bring an end to violence?
8. Why is this important?
9. What are the most helpful things you learned from this scenario?
10. How will you act differently as an RA, based on this new knowledge?

Resources

National Youth Violence Prevention Resource Center
http://www.safeyouth.org/scripts/index.asp
Assessing Potentially Violent Students
http://www.ericdigests.org/2000-3/violent.htm
CDC Violence Prevention Site
http://www.cdc.gov/ncipc/dvp/bestpractices.htm
AMA Violence Prevention Site
http://www.ama-assn.org/ama/pub/category/3242.html

Tips on Violence

1. Violence can escalate quickly.
2. Intervene early, even if residents believe you are "overreacting."
3. Have a zero tolerance policy toward violence.
4. Remember that words can be violent just as actions can be.
5. Never intervene in a violent situation by yourself; get help from a fellow staff member, supervisor, or police.

CONCLUSION

Reflecting on the Importance of the Work We Do

Few roles on the college campus are as important as that of the Resident Assistant. Who else lives, works, and learns with so many students so closely? Your role is among the most critical on campus. With the importance of your role comes much responsibility (as you know)! Here are a few concluding thoughts for you to ponder as you seek the best ways to make a difference with your residents.

First, I urge you to work toward bringing a renewed sense of the importance of ethics to your residents, and the other students with whom you interact. Part of your role as an RA is to be the conscience of your hall. It is a role that you can take as an opportunity to apply to your many leadership roles in the future. Clearly, we need more people who know how to behave in an ethical fashion throughout society.

One of the greatest legacies you can leave with your residents is to help them do a better job of defining a personal code of ethics that will guide them through their future. RAs are in the ideal place to work with students who make the inevitable errors in judgment that come with being a young adult. It is the RA who lives right there and can remind residents that their behavior reflects their code of ethics, and few things in life are more important than behaving with a high code of ethics.

One of the greatest challenges you will face in helping your residents behave in an ethical manner is to help them identify when an issue they face has ethical implications. If all of us in residence life spend more time helping students recognize an ethical dilemma when it exists, and teaching them how to ask good ethical questions, we can leave our residents with valuable tools to help them navigate their complex futures. A wise man once said that every complex problem has a simple solution that is wrong. The "wrong" simple solution to helping your residents learn how to ask good ethical questions is to try to give them the answers. As you interact with your residents, at the opportune moments, ask them:

- What are the ethical implications of your behavior?
- What are the ethical implications of that idea?
- What would be the consequence if everyone behaved that way?
- What then if everyone believed as you do?

Maybe you have a resident who talks about turning in a receipt to a student organization he belongs to for "just $40 worth" of personal expenses. As an educator, as an RA, you have the chance right then to make a teachable moment out of his mistake in judgment. Why do so? Because these kinds of behaviors can lead to habits and behaviors that can slowly lead him into patterns that one day lead him to be the next misguided auditor of a multinational corporation. Remember that the work you do every day has great consequences for the individuals who live on your floor, both now and after they graduate.

Reflecting for Perspective

As this book comes to a close, I hope you will join me on a thought exercise of sorts. You could just skip over this section, or not take it seriously if you choose. I hope you choose to take a minute to do some quiet reflection. So find a quiet, comfortable spot, and after you do, continue reading.

Now that you are comfortable, take a minute and think about who you are as a member of your college community. Think for just a minute about what you like the best about the college you attend.

Now think for a few minutes about what you like, enjoy, or hope to enjoy most about being an RA. Maybe it is a person you will be or were there for, or a lesson you learned or hope to learn in the coming year.

Think for awhile about how fortunate you are just to be able to go to college. Think then about how out of all the students on campus, you were the one who was chosen to lead your particular group of residents.

Your school could just put up a bunch of buildings for students to live in, but no, they believe in doing more than that. They know how important it is for students to have trained leaders and role models for other students who live near them. They know that you will do a great job. They know that you will make a huge difference in the lives of many, many people.

So knowing that, should you just sit back, think about how great it is that you have your job as an RA, how great it is that you are helping to educate those who will lead our nation into the future, and just feel good about yourself and where you are? Well, you do indeed have a lot to feel good about. However, a danger facing you is that you might become complacent. You might figure that everything will fall into place, you can just coast on through the year and everything will be OK. And indeed, you might have an OK year. Or, you can make the decision, right now, to make your time ahead as an RA the most memorable year of your life so far. You can decide you are going to live up to and exceed all the expectations you and your school have for you in the year ahead. You can choose to show your residents that you are not afraid to make a difference, you can show your fellow staff members that you are a contributing part of a dynamic team that together builds the best community possible, you can prove to yourself that you had it in you all along, that you took each challenge this year as an opportunity to have an effect on people's lives, and you can finish the year with a warm glow in your heart knowing that you did the best you could and your best was great.

How do you do this? Tackle every challenge you face head on, all year, with all you've got. If you see fellow staff members not getting along, help them work it out. If you hear a resident make a comment that hurts other people, find the right time to have a good conversation about it. If you see a need, ask yourself how you can help instead of asking who else might take care of it. When others can help you, ask for their advice, support, and assistance early on. Look around you and see the great potential in others, see the opportunities to change things for the better, to share yourself with your fellow students.

Like many leaders, I'm willing to bet that you want to believe in something, that you are a part of doing something great. You want to believe that what you do matters, and that you matter as a person. Being an RA gives you the chance to do all of that. You can believe in the educational power of living in community. You can believe in your role and your ability to create the strongest community possible among your residents. You can know that every time you challenge or support a resident that you are helping them grow, and helping them to become a better person who will then affect the lives of many people in the future.

As someone who used to be an RA, and now a "fellow RA" of yours, I close with a personal anecdote. As a kid, I always thought that I could change the world. I have never given up on that goal. I hope in some way it is a dream that you share as well. Knowing that you are or will soon be an RA, I'm sure there is a big part of that dream within you. Personally, I believe in the core of my being that each one of us can change the world. We don't have to change every life in the world, or even every life at our college or university to have a significant impact on our college and the world around us. A few times when I have shared that dream, to change the world, with others I'll hear a snicker, an obnoxious comment, or an excuse for a norm of mediocrity. If and when you ever hear such a response to your desire to change the world, please remember this quote:

> Don't ever let anyone tell you that "you can't change the world," for such is the rally cry of the cynics and the unambitious.

Read that quote again, and again when someone tries to get you down.

If any of us believe that we alone can change the world, honestly, we deceive ourselves. I certainly don't believe that I can change the world alone. I do believe that we can change the world together. In the context of the work that we all do, together, we change the world one resident at a time, one floor at a time, one suite at a time, one apartment at a time, one residence hall at a time, one university at a time, and together we make a difference in one nation at a time and beyond.

Give all you can to your role. Make it a year to remember. Live by the principles that will create a sense of camaraderie among your staff and among your residents that you will always point to as an ideal community. In doing so, you give your residents memories that last a lifetime. You leave them with lessons on how to relate well with others, lessons about who they are as individuals, and help them develop the skills it will take for them to lead a part of the world when they leave. And by the end of the year, you can know that you did all you could to make a difference, and with your staff you created something you can be proud of, together.

May the year ahead be one that you can look back on with a deep sense of accomplishment, knowing that you did all you could to make a difference in others, and at the same time, made a big difference in the person that is you.

What is *Your* Story?

Do you have a lesson you learned during your experience as an RA that you would like to share? Do you have an experience you believe other RAs could learn from? Did you make a big mistake that you hope others won't repeat? If so, why not share it with others? We are now collecting stories for a forthcoming second edition of *Lessons Learned*. Tell us about that time you really blew it. Tell us about the time you fell flat on your face as a staff member, but picked yourself up and made a difference. Write a letter like the ones you've seen in this book, and e-mail it to Foubert@wm.edu. You can also send authored or anonymous submissions to Dr. John Foubert, the College of William and Mary, School of Education, PO Box 8795, Williamsburg, VA 23187-8795.

Ask Dr. John

Are you facing a tough situation in your role as an RA, and you aren't sure what to do? Have you hit a brick wall and don't know what to try next? Do you just need a word of encouragement to keep going? Ask Dr. John! Dr. John Foubert, the author of this book, is happy to respond to your e-mailed questions and thoughts. Just send an e-mail to Foubert@wm.edu. Of course, the best source of advice for you is your supervisor and other administrators and faculty at your school, but if you want an outside perspective, just send "Dr. John" an e-mail and he will give you his thoughts on the challenge you face.

Index

A

Academically struggling students,
69–72
Alcohol, 12, 99–103, 105–109,
121–128

B

Budgets, 161–164

C

Community colleges, 73–76
Confidentiality, 133–137, 183–186
Conflict
    Importance of confronting early,
        17–21
    Online, 61–65, 87–90
    With another staff member,
        179–182
Counseling, 133–137, 139–142,
    195–200
Cults, 29–33
Cutting, 149–152

D

Delegating tasks, 11–15
Domestic violence, 115–119
Drug use, 125–128

E

Eating Disorders, 139–142
Ecstasy, 125–128

F

Facebook, 61–65
Fire alarm, 191–194
First-Year students, 3–6, 91–95,
    133–137

G

Getting fired, 161–163, 173–177

H

Hall council, 11–15
Hall furniture, 87–90

I

Illegal drugs, 125–128
Instant Messenger, 87–90

L

Language
    Anti-gay, 49
    Hate speech, 49
    Politically correct, 50
    Racist, 43–48, 49
    Hate speech, 49

M

Money, 161–163

O

Online harassment, 201–205
Open door policy, 3–6
Over-involved residents, 73–76

P

Panic attack, 153–156
Parents
　　Asking for your phone number,
　　　　83–86
　　Calling you, 83–86
　　Confidentiality, 183–186
　　Setting boundaries, 83–86
Policy violations
　　Alcohol, 12, 99–103, 121–124
　　Consistency, 111–114
　　Documenting, 99–103, 105–109,
　　　　111–114, 121–124, 125–128
　　Enforcement, 121–124, 165–168,
　　　　173–177
　　Fire alarms, 191–194
　　Furniture, 87–90
　　Ignoring, 99–103
　　Noise, 105–109
Programming
　　Cookouts, 11–15, 111
　　Creative ideas, 7–10
　　Planning, 23–28

R

Race
　　Eating in dining hall, 44

Racism, 43–48, 111–114
　　Stereotypes, 37–41
　　Tension, 37–54
Religion, 29–33
Religious differences, 55–59
Residents
　　Abuse from, 105–109
　　Availability to, 3–6, 91–95
　　Dating them, 169–172
　　Drinking alcohol with, 173–177
　　As friends, 91–95
　　Lonely, 29–33, 69–72, 77–81
Roommates, 30, 78, 122, 144, 196,
　　　　202

S

Self-mutilation, 143–147, 149–152
Service learning, 23–28
Sexual assault, 25, 195–200
Student athletes, 69–72, 87–90
Suicide, 133–137, 201–205

T

Technology, 61–65

V

Vandalism, 77–78
Violence, 115–119, 207–211